Diseases and Disorders

Anorexia and Bulimia

Titles in the Diseases and Disorders series include:

Alzheimer's Disease
Attention Deficit Disorder
Autism
Breast Cancer
Down Syndrome
Epilepsy
Learning Disabilities
Phobias
Schizophrenia

Diseases and Disorders

Anorexia and Bulimia

by Alison Cotter

Library of Congress Cataloging-in-Publication Data

Cotter, Alison, 1963–
    Anorexia and bulimia / by Alison Cotter.
    p. ; cm. — (Diseases and disorders)
Includes bibliographical references and index.
Summary: Discusses the eating disorders anorexia and bulimia including history and research, psychological and biological causes, societal pressures, treatment, recovery, and prevention.
    ISBN 1-56006-725-X (hardback : alk. paper)
    1. Anorexia nervosa—Juvenile literature. 2. Bulimia—Juvenile literature. [1. Anorexia nervosa. 2. Bulimia. 3. Eating disorders.]
    [DNLM: 1. Anorexia Nervosa—Juvenile Literature. 2. Bulimia—Juvenile Literature. WM 175 C847a 2001] I. Title. II. Diseases and disorders series
    RC552.A5 C67 2002
    616.85'26—dc21

00-012858

Table of Contents

"The Most Difficult Puzzles Ever Devised"

CHARLES BEST, ONE of the pioneers in the search for a cure for diabetes, once explained what it is about medical research that intrigued him so. "It's not just the gratification of knowing one is helping people," he confided, "although that probably is a more heroic and selfless motivation. Those feelings may enter in, but truly, what I find best is the feeling of going toe to toe with nature, of trying to solve the most difficult puzzles ever devised. The answers are there somewhere, those keys that will solve the puzzle and make the patient well. But how will those keys be found?"

Since the dawn of civilization, nothing has so puzzled people—and often frightened them, as well—as the onset of illness in a body or mind that had seemed healthy before. A seizure, the inability of a heart to pump, the sudden deterioration of muscle tone in a small child—being unable to reverse such conditions or even to understand why they occur was unspeakably frustrating to healers. Even before there were names for such conditions, even before they were understood at all, each was a reminder of how complex the human body was, and how vulnerable.

While our grappling with understanding diseases has been frustrating at times, it has also provided some of humankind's most heroic accomplishments. Alexander Fleming's accidental discovery in 1928 of a mold that could be turned into penicillin has resulted in the saving of untold millions of lives. The isolation of the enzyme insulin has reversed what was once a death sentence for anyone with diabetes. There have been great strides in combating conditions for which there is not yet a cure, too. Medicines can help AIDS patients live longer, diagnostic tools such as mammography and ultrasounds can help doctors find tumors while they are treatable, and laser surgery techniques have made the most intricate, minute operations routine.

This "toe-to-toe" competition with diseases and disorders is even more remarkable when seen in a historical continuum. An astonishing amount of progress has been made in a very short time. Just two hundred years ago, the existence of germs as a cause of some diseases was unknown. In fact, it was less than 150 years ago that a British surgeon named Joseph Lister had difficulty persuading his fellow doctors that washing their hands before delivering a baby might increase the chances of a healthy delivery (especially if they had just attended to a diseased patient)!

Each book in Lucent's *Diseases and Disorders* series explores a disease or disorder and the knowledge that has been accumulated (or discarded) by doctors through the years. Each book also examines the tools used for pinpointing a diagnosis, as well as the various means that are used to treat or cure a disease. Finally, new ideas are presented—techniques or medicines that may be on the horizon.

Frustration and disappointment are still part of medicine, for not every disease or condition can be cured or prevented. But the limitations of knowledge are being pushed outward constantly; the "most difficult puzzles ever devised" are finding challengers every day.

Knowledge is the Best Defense

Anorexia and bulimia are the two most commonly known types of eating disorders. People develop anorexia and bulimia out of a desire to lose weight. Though many people around the world diet or exercise to lose weight, most do not progress to the point of developing anorexia and bulimia. What separates anorexics and bulimics from the general population is that their desire to control their weight ends up controlling them. They find that they cannot break the dangerous habits associated with these illnesses, such as refusing to eat to the point of starvation, vomiting after meals, or abusing laxatives. Eventually these habits cause serious physical damage that can lead to hospitalization or even death.

Disorders with Unclear Causes

Although doctors are able to treat the physical damage caused by anorexia and bulimia, they do not yet know what causes these disorders. Therefore no medication exists to prevent anorexia and bulimia or to cure it once it develops. It is thought that a combination of factors contributes to the development of anorexia and bulimia. These include biological, psychological, and societal factors. Doctors have found that they are able to help patients control anorexia and bulimia primarily through therapy, which addresses the psychological causes. However, if a biological cause can be identified, experts believe that a cure might one day be available.

Continued research into the causes of anorexia and bulimia has led to other discoveries as well. Once thought to be a problem that affected only teens and, in particular, teenage girls, anorexia and bulimia are now thought to be widespread among boys as well as specific groups, such as athletes. Experts have also found some cases of eating disorders to be closely linked to depression, a risk factor for suicide. In fact, according to the American Psychiatric Association, anorexia has one of the highest-known death rates of any psychiatric disorder: One percent of teenage girls in the United States develops the disease and up to 10 percent of those diagnosed with it die as a result.

Living in Secret

Many anorexics and bulimics, though, manage to keep their illness a secret. In fact, anorexics and bulimics often live in fear of

Doctors do not yet know what causes anorexia and bulimia, although they speculate that a combination of biological, psychological, and societal factors contributes to the development of the disorders.

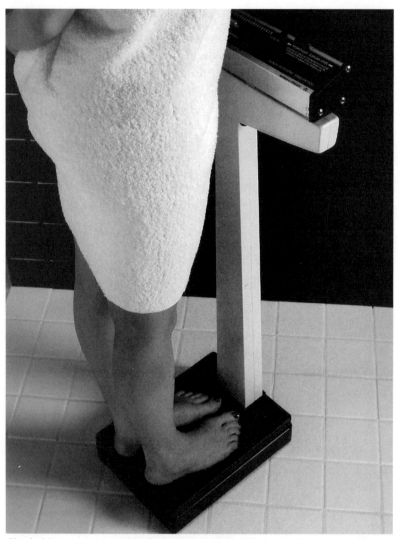

The habits anorexics and bulimics use to control their weight, such as refusing to eat or purging, become difficult to break.

someone discovering their illness and go to great lengths to hide their symptoms. They may wear baggy clothes to cover up their skeletal bodies or lie about having eaten. An anorexic, for example, may tell her parents that she ate at a friend's house or at the mall when she actually has not eaten all day. In this way anorexics and bulimics prolong their illness and decrease their chances of recovery because the dangerous habits they have developed become harder and harder to break. And the longer they don't eat, or purge what they have eaten, the higher their risk of doing irreversible damage to their bodies.

Until a cure for anorexia and bulimia can be found, it seems that public awareness is the best defense. The more the public knows about the dangers of eating disorders, their warning signs, and their possible causes, the better able people will be to fight them. One outcome of the growing public awareness is that more and more teens are admitting that they know someone from their *own* school or their *own* circle of friends who shows signs of an eating disorder. Armed with this knowledge, then, doctors, experts, parents, and teens themselves hope fewer young people will develop these dangerous disorders.

Chapter 1

What Are Anorexia and Bulimia?

A LTHOUGH ANOREXIA AND bulimia typically occur in teenage girls who are desperate to be thin, these disorders can strike anyone who is overly concerned about their weight, including males, athletes, the elderly, and children. People who develop the disorders often begin by dieting, although dieting itself if done properly is not dangerous. Millions of people follow healthy diets and exercise regularly to lose weight and stay in shape. Some, however, go too far, and people who develop anorexia and bulimia use extreme measures to stay thin. Many become so thin that their bodies cannot function normally. Some need to be hospitalized as a result, and some even die.

Anorexia

The term *anorexia* is of Greek origin. "An" means "lack of" and "orexis" means "appetite." Put simply, people who suffer from anorexia have no desire to eat. Often, people lose their appetite when they have a headache, are depressed, or are suffering from an illness like cancer. However, with anorexia, the loss of appetite is usually unexplainable. Often an appetite exists, but the anorexic simply refuses to eat or limits meals to very small quantities of food. Historian Joan Jacobs Brumberg of Cornell University, who studies eating disorders, reports that an anorexic "may limit herself to between 200 and 400 calories a day"[1] which is alarmingly low considering that the average teen needs more than 2,000 to grow and stay healthy.

Anorexics refuse food or limit how much they eat because they fear gaining weight. Many want to lose weight even when they are already thin. In fact, doctors usually define anorexia in terms of a person's weight, as opposed to in terms of a person's appetite. Anorexia is viewed as a refusal to maintain weight rather than simply a refusal to eat. A diagnosis of anorexia, too, is based on weight. *Consumers' Research* food editor Beatrice Trum Hunter writes that "typically, an anorexic refuses to maintain weight that is above the lowest weight considered to be normal for the person's age and height, and the total body weight is at least 15% below normal."[2]

Outwardly anorexics might appear to be successful and even healthy. They are typically people who are intelligent, independent, admired by their peers, and overachievers. Sixteen-year-old Martha, who plays on her high school tennis team and gets

Anorexics take exercising and dieting to the extreme.

straight A's, is a typical example. Martha recalls that friends were impressed with her healthy diet of salads and fruits. What her friends did not know was that she ate nothing but salads and fruit and ate them in quantities too small to give her body adequate nutrition. Some anorexics also begin to exercise, which is traditionally used to burn excess calories. In the case of anorexics, however, it is used to burn *essential* calories. Martha, for example, started a daily routine of sit-ups, leg lifts, and jumping jacks, a regimen that further taxed her already weak body. Based on age and height, Martha's ideal body weight should have been 125 pounds, yet Martha was hospitalized at the age of fourteen, weighing just 69 pounds.

Identifying someone with anorexia is not always easy. Anorexics may wear loose-fitting clothes to hide the fact that they are losing too much weight. Martha's mother first became seriously concerned about her daughter's eating habits when they went clothes shopping. When Martha took off her clothes to try on a dress, her mother was shocked to see that she was just skin and bones. Furthermore, according to B. Timothy Walsh, M.D., a professor of psychiatry at Columbia University and director of the Eating Disorder Research Unit of the New York State Psychiatric Institute, "Anorexics are not always startlingly underweight."[3] Dr. Walsh says that anorexics are sometimes just thin enough to look good in clothes. These anorexics—along with society in general—believe they look normal because their perception of normal is based on fashions worn by models who are usually too thin as well. The fact that society accepts being too thin as normal is part of the reason why anorexia is sometimes misdiagnosed or missed altogether.

From Simple Diet to Deadly Obsession

Anorexics become obsessed with counting and, more important, cutting calories. Yet their obsession often begins as a simple diet. Again, Martha's case is typical. She started to pay close attention to what she ate and how much she weighed. After a while it was all she could think about. Another teen named Wendy, who was

Many anorexics are not noticeably underweight, and loose-fitting clothes can hide those who are.

teased about being overweight, began dieting in the eighth grade. Over time, she gave up candy, then fat, then meat. The five-foot, six-inch-tall teen went from 145 pounds to 84 pounds in eighteen months. Wendy says she got to the point where she was just "drinking water, eating cucumbers and other vegetables, and chewing gum"[4] to curb her appetite.

'For heaven's sake Jackie, forget the diet for one day.'

Although anorexics claim to have no interest in food, they actually think about eating all the time as part of their obsession. They may talk about food constantly, read about food in magazines and cookbooks, or make trips to the grocery store to simply look at food. Or they may even take an interest in buying food and cooking for others, but not for themselves. One teen recalls, "I was obsessed with food. I would cook and cook and cook, but not eat."[5] Many doctors believe that anorexics satisfy their own hunger by feeding others. It is also a way to test themselves—offering food but not taking any gives them a sense of superiority.

Along with obsessive thoughts about food comes overwhelming guilt about eating. Although anorexics constantly feel hungry, they pride themselves on their ability to control that desire. They believe that allowing themselves to eat is a weakness. Some take it a step further, convincing themselves that they don't deserve to eat. Martha remembers dreaming about food and waking up with feelings of shame for having eaten just one dream cookie. Even after she started treatment for her anorexia, Martha continued to be haunted by guilt. In her journal she wrote: "At breakfast I didn't finish my milk, cottage cheese, or eat the raisins in my cereal, yet I still feel guilty for what I did eat. My mind is totally food-oriented. I can't think of anything else."[6]

Mind over Matter

As a result, anorexics develop an incredible sense of willpower. Even though their stomachs constantly tell them to eat, their brains tell them not to eat because they fear that if they let themselves eat in a moment of weakness they might not be able to stop, and they worry too that eating will lead to their getting fat. In fact, people who suffer from anorexia think they are already

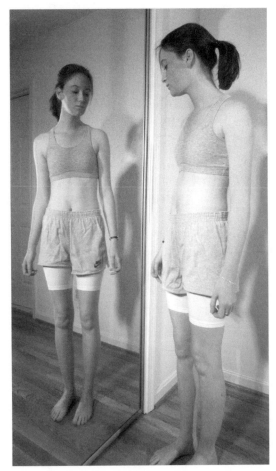

People who suffer from anorexia have a distorted view of themselves, believing they are fat when they are not.

fat, even when they are not. They have what doctors say is a distorted view of themselves and of what makes the *ideal* body. Martha, for instance, remembers thinking that her emaciated body looked normal. Another teen recalls, "When people said I looked skeletal, I was secretly pleased. Even as I was admitted to the hospital at age 14, I thought they were just jealous of my willpower."[7]

Though anorexics have slowly learned to control their desire for food, many who suffer from the illness say they actually feel on the verge of losing control. Martha felt that food was consuming her life. Her days revolved around thinking about food and ways to avoid eating—two activities at basic odds with one another. The stress became too much. Martha recalls, "I didn't feel like a normal person. I felt like I was going [crazy]."[8] What began as a desire to control her weight became an out-of-control compulsion—one that ultimately ended up controlling her. When a victim reaches this point they often require therapy or, if they are in medical danger, hospitalization in order to regain control of their thoughts as well as their lives.

Bulimia

Bulimia is a more common eating disorder than anorexia and it can also go undetected for years. In fact, when anorexics are no longer able to control their desire for food, they often turn to bulimia as a way to continue to control their weight. Bulimia is thought to be prevalent among college-age women. Anorexia Nervosa and Related Eating Disorders, Inc. (ANRED) reports that about 4 percent, or four out of one hundred college-age women are bulimic. Other sources claim that the rate of bulimia among college-age women is much higher, between 25 to 30 percent.

The term *bulimia* comes from Latin and means "hunger of an ox." Bulimics seem to have a huge appetite—the hunger of an ox—but they do not gain weight from constantly overeating. Unlike anorexics, who refuse to eat or limit what they do eat to very small quantities, bulimics let themselves eat and, often, eat large quantities of food. This is called binge eating or simply bingeing.

They avoid gaining weight by what doctors refer to as purging. Methods of purging include secretly vomiting or misusing laxatives, enemas, diuretics, or other medications to help the body quickly eliminate food. Whereas anorexics are proud of their ability to control their desire to eat, bulimics are usually ashamed and embarrassed about their lack of control.

Eating in Secret

Bulimics usually eat in secret, consuming food in quantities far greater than that of normal meals. Often they find the most unhealthy foods to be the most satisfying and are not able to limit themselves to one serving. Instead they might eat a whole box of cookies, a pint of ice cream, or an entire bag of chips. One woman reported that when the feeling of hunger struck, she would run to the fridge and eat anything she could get her hands on, including just dipping a finger into a jar of mayonnaise. Another ate from a stash of cookies and candy she kept hidden under her bed. According to Brumberg, bulimics "may ingest as much as 8,000 calories in one sitting."[9] Those who are considered bulimic binge and purge at least twice a week over a period of at least three months.

Bulimia is similar to anorexia in a number of ways. For example, it is also hard to identify people who are bulimic. They are not necessarily thin and many maintain an average weight. Bulimics usually appear to eat a balanced diet and lead a normal lifestyle, even though they continue to purge their food in secret. Also like anorexia, bulimia often develops out of a simple desire to lose a few pounds but eventually gets out of control. Many bulimics say they feel possessed by their illness: They can't stop themselves from eating once they start, and they can't stop themselves from purging once they've eaten. Their way of controlling food consumption actually ends up controlling their lives, sometimes to the point of bingeing and purging up to eighteen times a day.

Furthermore, like anorexics, bulimics also experience an overwhelming sense of guilt after eating. Purging what they've eaten is a way of getting rid of the guilt. One female athlete who vomited

Bulimics binge in secret, ashamed of their lack of control.

after meals recalls, "My whole insides burned, it was the worst feeling, but afterward there was a sense of relief. I felt my stomach go down a little bit."[10]

The visible evidence—the thrown-up food, the flatter tummy—gives bulimics a sense of accomplishment and relieves their guilt. What many bulimics do not realize is that the bingeing and purging habit is actually very harmful to the body. It can damage the teeth and throat as well as lead to serious medical complications such as dehydration, irregular heartbeat, and kidney damage.

Typical Sufferers of Anorexia and Bulimia

According to *Time* magazine, 2 million people in the United States have an eating disorder, a small number compared to the number who suffer from other deadly diseases like cancer or AIDS. However, eating disorder specialist Carolyn Costin believes that "cases of eating disorders are probably underreported, due to the connection of these disorders to fear and shame."[11] Moreover, doctors cannot track anorexia and bulimia the way they track other life-threatening illnesses. Signs of cancer, for example, show up on peoples' skin or in X rays, but those suffering from eating disorders are often very careful to hide the signs of their illness. People who have eating disorders usually seek help from a doctor only after the disorder has caused physical problems. Current statistics are based on the number of people who seek treatment or become hospitalized, but it is thought that many more may endure these disorders in silence.

Eating Disorders Typically Found in White Females

From the available statistics, experts have identified particular at-risk groups. Traditionally, eating disorders occur most often in white, middle- to upper-middle-class young women. Experts speculate that one reason may be that being thin is particularly important to women in middle- to upper-middle-class families. For example, one study found that many college-age women (from such homes and in general) evaluate other women, themselves, and their own achievements in terms of weight. However, recent studies have shown that the average age of teens suffering from anorexia and bulimia has dropped from sixteen or seventeen to fourteen, with some even younger. Barbara Fleming, coordinator for the National Eating Disorders Organization in Tulsa, Oklahoma, says, "We used to

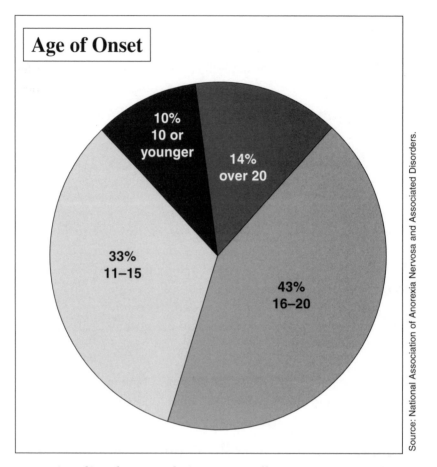

Age of Onset

10%
10 or younger

14%
over 20

33%
11–15

43%
16–20

see eating disorders mostly in young college-age women. Now it's not unusual for kids in elementary and middle school to become anorexic or bulimic."[12]

Statistics tend to support Fleming's assertion. In a 1995 study of three hundred children conducted by Children's Hospital Medical Center of Cincinnati, Ohio, 29 percent of third-grade boys and 39 percent of third-grade girls said they had dieted; 60 percent of sixth-grade girls and 31 percent of sixth-grade boys reported trying to lose weight. Experts contend that this kind of early concern about one's appearance can lead to the development of an eating disorder, one that may begin in elementary school but may not become apparent to parents or friends until much later.

Other Ethnic Groups

The focus on eating disorders among white females has led researchers to believe that white females are more likely than females in other ethnic groups to be dissatisfied with their bodies. For example, the journal *Science* mentions research conducted in 1996 in which black women, who do not commonly develop eating disorders, were found to express less dissatisfaction with their bodies than white women of similar weight.

However, some researchers say these statistics aren't accurate. They argue that more cases of eating disorders are found in middle- to upper-middle-class white females simply because that is where researchers are looking. These critics believe that further study of eating disorders among other ethnic groups is needed to better educate the public and the medical community about who might be at risk for developing eating disorders. As early as 1993, *Essence* magazine journalist Maya Browne reported that incidences of both anorexia and bulimia were on the rise in the black community. "The myth that Black culture protects Black women from all eating disorders except obesity is still prevalent within the medical community. And most people believe that bulimia and anorexia are white people's problems."[13]

Other research has focused on the Hispanic and Asian population. For example, researchers at the Stanford Center for Research in Disease Prevention compared the rate of body dissatisfaction among white, Hispanic, and Asian adolescent girls in Northern California. The girls answered questions about their desired body shape as well as their parents' body shape to determine what factors are associated with body dissatisfaction and how they differ among whites, Hispanics, and Asians. The researchers assumed that white girls would have greater body dissatisfaction than Hispanic and Asian girls, but actually found that Hispanic girls were significantly more dissatisfied with their bodies than white girls. In terms of what each group perceives to be the ideal body shape, the researchers found little difference among the white, Hispanic, and Asian girls. The researchers concluded, then, that "body dissatisfaction is not limited to middle-class and upper-class white

girls, and the same risk factors are associated with body dissatisfaction across ethnic groups."[14]

The researchers also said, "We studied body dissatisfaction as
a measure of disorder eating attitudes and a potential precursor
of disordered eating behaviors."[15] However, body dissatisfaction
does not automatically lead to what doctors call "clinical" cases

Although some researchers believe eating disorders are most common among
middle-to-upper class white women, others have found that minority women
are also at risk.

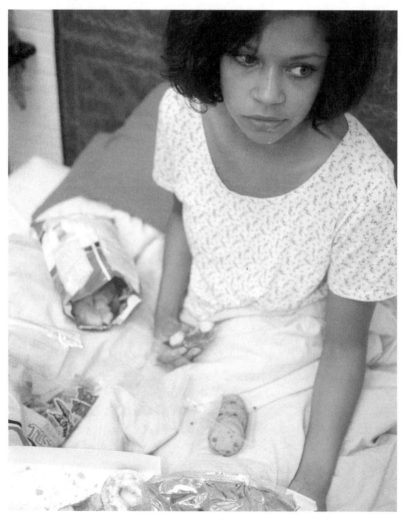

of eating disorders. (A case is considered "clinical" when a person has been officially diagnosed with anorexia or bulimia, as opposed to someone just suspected of having one of these disorders.) Attitudes toward weight and appearance that children learn from their parents as well as from the media and culture play a role. Further, cultural environments vary among different ethnic groups and even among families within each ethnic group. The researchers noted that in some cases an adolescent's environment may help prevent the development of clinical eating disorders. In others it may help promote this development. That is why determining the causes of anorexia and bulimia is such a challenge.

Eating Disorders Now Found in Males

Just as some ethnic groups may be underrepresented when it comes to studying eating disorders, so are males. Experts have found that concerns about weight and appearance are not exclusive to girls. Although eating disorders are more commonly found among girls, anorexia and bulimia among adolescent and teenage boys is also an issue. According to Anorexia Nervosa and Related Eating Disorders, Inc. (ANRED), about 5 to 10 percent of people who have anorexia and bulimia are male. Since 1995, reported cases of males with anorexia and bulimia have been steadily increasing, yet the reason for the rise is not clear. *Newsweek* reporter Jean Seligmann says, "Researchers don't know if there are more new cases of eating disorders in men—or simply more recognition."[16]

There are some similarities in how males and females are afflicted with eating disorders, but there are also many differences. Both genders can develop symptoms of eating disorders during adolescence, for example. However, in females the symptoms usually occur during puberty, according to University of Iowa psychiatrist Dr. Arnold Andersen, who has treated more than 1,000 girls and women and about 120 men with eating disorders. Conversely, Andersen found that symptoms occurred later in males—in late adolescence or their early twenties. Furthermore, whereas anorexia in females is often a reaction to the development of breasts and

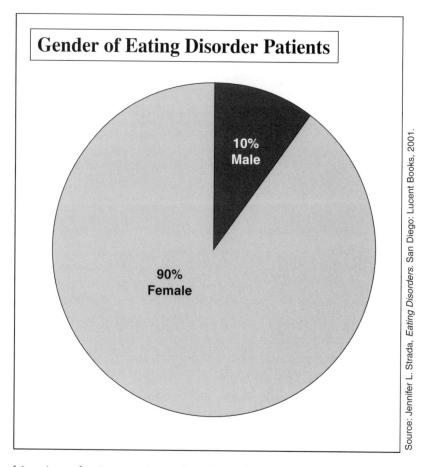

Gender of Eating Disorder Patients

10%
Male

90%
Female

Source: Jennifer L. Strada, *Eating Disorders*. San Diego: Lucent Books, 2001.

hips, in males it sometimes signals confusion over sexual orientation; Andersen says "about 22 percent of men with anorexia are homosexual."[17] However, other studies have shown that homosexuality is frequently but not necessarily associated with eating disorders among men. No one knows for sure.

There are also differences in how males and females are afflicted with eating disorders. For example, eating disorders among females are more widespread compared to males where eating disorders tend to be limited to certain groups such as models, actors, gymnasts, wrestlers, and jockeys. Eating disorders in males can also manifest themselves in a completely different way than in females. For example, compulsive running has come to be regarded as the male counterpart to female anorexia, although young women can become compulsive runners, too. Interestingly, compulsive runners and anorexics have similar characteristics. For example, both tend to be high achievers from affluent families.

Eating Disorders Among Athletes

A special area of concern is eating disorders among athletes. Just as females tend to be the focus of research concerning eating disorders among the general population, they are also the focus of research concerning eating disorders among athletes. This is because the rate of eating disorders among female athletes compared to nonathletes is so high. According to Katherine Fulkerson, Ph.D., a clinical psychologist who specializes in eating disorders, "Eating disorders are more common among female athletes than in the general population, as high as 60 percent in sports in which low body weight or ideal body shape confer, or are perceived to confer, an advantage."[18]

Gymnastics, figure skating, and ballet are considered high-risk sports for eating disorders. In fact, in a *Sports Illustrated* special report on eating disorders, reporter Merrell Noden notes, "The average size of the women on the U.S. Olympic gymnastic team has shrunk from 5'3" 105 pounds in 1976 to 4'9" 88 pounds in 1992."[19]

Even so, researchers have also found that eating disorders are beginning to occur in sports outside the risk zone. They also found that eating disorders are no longer exclusive to elite athletes or to females. Serious cases of anorexia and bulimia are occurring at the college and high school level as well as in male athletes.

In an article for *Teen* magazine on athletes and eating disorders, Alison Bell reported that "In a survey of 182 varsity-level female athletes conducted by researchers at Michigan State University, 32 percent said that they had used one unhealthy method to lose weight."[20] The study further showed that even athletes participating in sports that have no weight restrictions such as field hockey, tennis, softball, volleyball, and cheerleading can develop eating disorders and that the problem of eating disorders among athletes is much more widespread than originally believed.

Ballet is considered a high-risk sport for eating disorders because low body weight is considered essential for success.

A Slowly Developing Disorder

Anorexia and bulimia are serious disorders that affect thousands of young people each year, not just white girls from upper-class families as previously thought, but girls and boys from all walks of life and a variety of ethnic backgrounds. Anorexia and bulimia do not "strike" people the way illnesses like cancer do. Instead, anorexia and bulimia develop slowly over time, usually out of a simple desire to lose weight that eventually becomes an uncontrollable obsession. People who suffer from anorexia and bulimia often go to great lengths to hide their illness from family and friends. In fact, many suffer in silence, sometimes for years, before the devastating physical effects of their illness are discovered by their family or physician. If untreated, anorexia and bulimia can cause serious medical complications and, possibly, even death.

Chapter 2

Psychological and Biological Causes

A NOREXIA AND BULIMIA are generally thought to result from certain emotional and psychological problems. Some of the problems most commonly linked to these disorders include low self-esteem, depression, and stress from traumatic situations such as divorce or death. Some researchers think the roots of anorexia and bulimia may go deeper than this, however. New research has targeted possible biological causes, including certain brain chemical imbalances. Results are encouraging, but no exact cause has yet been identified for anorexia or bulimia. Regarding anorexia, Dr. B. Timothy Walsh says, "At the moment, we accept that we do not know, in any very specific way, what causes this to develop and why, once it has begun, it is sometimes so persistent."[21]

Distorted Self-Image

People who suffer from anorexia and bulimia often see themselves as healthy even though they are sick. They look in the mirror, see their thin reflection, and believe they look good even though they may be dangerously underweight. One anorexic woman, at six feet tall, weighed only one hundred pounds. She was so skinny that even lying in bed was uncomfortable because she had no muscle to support her body and was just lying on her skeleton. Yet, when she looked at her skeletal body in the mirror, she thought, "Part of me thinks I like what I see."[22] The skinnier she got, the more beautiful she felt—and the less she thought she needed help.

Often anorexics and bulimics have a distorted image of themselves. They believe they would look better if they lost more weight. Some even believe they look fat because the image they see in the mirror is distorted. Eating disorder therapist Lisa Selzman, who works with anorexics and bulimics, describes having an eating disorder as similar to being in a carnival fun house, something that is appealing on the outside but frightening on the inside. Selzman says, "Your image in the mirrors is horribly distorted, and it's hard to find your way out."[23]

Lack of Self-Esteem

The reason that it is hard to find the way out is that anorexia and bulimia are thought to be physical expressions of other, more deeply rooted psychological problems such as a lack of self-esteem (also referred to as a lack of sense of self). According to eating disorder specialist Carolyn Costin, "Eating disorders are not about food or weight but about a disordered 'sense of self' looking for approval and finding it, however temporarily, in the pursuit of thinness or the comfort of food."[24] Self-esteem is difficult to define. Someone with high self-esteem might be described as confident and self-assured. Most likely a person with high self-esteem was raised in a positive, loving environment. Conversely, children who are ignored, criticized, ridiculed, or abused will usually have less self-esteem and, possibly, a negative self-image.

Children who lack self-esteem grow up feeling inadequate and seeking approval from others. Often they develop negative feelings toward themselves which can lead to negative, sometimes uncontrollable, thoughts. One mother, Peggy Claude-Pierre, discovered that her anorexic daughter suffered from a deep-rooted sense of inadequacy. The daughter felt as though she didn't deserve to eat. In fact, the daughter described the situation as feeling like she had two minds, one that told her to eat and another that told her she wasn't good enough to eat. Claude-Pierre said, "[my daughter] told me there seemed to be

Children who suffer from low self-esteem and feelings of inadequacy often develop negative feelings about themselves which can lead to eating disorders.

some other, louder thought pattern in her head that made no logical sense."[25] Claude-Pierre's daughter likened the situation to a traffic light. She sees it is green and knows it means go, but her head tells her it is red and she stops. Though the young girl was fully aware that this pattern of thought made no sense, she was unable to control it.

Claude-Pierre helped her daughter overcome anorexia by slowly helping her learn to eat again. Of course, this required that the mother give her daughter a lot of special attention, and many psychologists argue that a need for attention due to lack of self-esteem is the underlying cause of anorexia and bulimia. Therefore, anorexia and bulimia could be considered just a way of getting attention. This might be especially true for teens who feel they are being ignored by their parents. On the other hand, teens who feel that their parents are overly involved in their lives might develop anorexia or bulimia as a form of escape. Carolyn Costin believes "Eating disorder symptoms are [confusing], in that they can be used as an expression of and defense against feelings and needs."[26]

A traumatic event such as a move to another city or the loss of a parent through divorce or death can also affect self-esteem and trigger anorexia or bulimia. One boy's parents separated when he was nine. His mother remarried and the boy moved to Germany when his new stepfather was transferred to another job. He was depressed and unhappy in Germany and started to watch what he ate. He also started to go to the gym with his stepfather to try to build up his muscles. With his mother busy with a new baby and his stepfather busy at work, the boy felt neglected and ate less and less. When he returned to the United States to visit, his father noticed his dramatic loss of weight and got help. The boy was admitted to a program at age thirteen, weighing only seventy-three pounds at five feet tall. Though his parents were not reunited over his condition, each realized that the boy needed much more of their attention. And, with the help of family therapy, the boy was eventually able to feel close to each parent again and overcome his disorder.

Perfectionism

Another psychological cause of anorexia and bulimia links the disease to certain personality types. For example, people who are considered perfectionists might be at greater risk for developing an eating disorder. Controlling calories, many doctors speculate, goes along with a perfectionist's need to control everything.

Sixteen-year-old Martha is a typical example. Martha plays on her high school tennis team, gets straight A's, and is a perfectionist; her room is always neat and the shoes in her closet are arranged by season. She started counting calories when she was thirteen years old. She says, "I figured, I weighed eighty pounds, why not be seventy-nine? I thought I was doing the right thing, improving myself."[27]

Research has shown that perfectionism is common among athletes, a group that is particularly at risk for developing eating disorders. Eating disorder specialist Carolyn Costin believes "Athletes have a predisposition to be perfectionists because that is part of what drives them to excel in a sport."[28] Athletes bent on "perfecting" their game often believe that slimming down will enhance

Studies have found that athletes are particularly at risk for eating disorders because many are perfectionists driven to excel at their sport.

A traumatic event can affect self-esteem and trigger anorexia or bulimia.

their performance. Female athletes in particular are developing a "be thin to win" attitude where being skinny is equated with being successful, just as it is in popular culture.

Children who are perfectionists often learned that behavior from their parents. In fact, researchers found that mothers who dieted out of their need to perfect their own bodies were twice as likely as nondieters to push their sons and daughters to do the same. One study conducted by Children's Hospital Medical Center of Cincinnati, Ohio, for instance, found eight-year-olds who were concerned about weight because their parents were concerned about it.

This pressure to be perfect can also lead to feelings of inadequacy. Mothers and fathers who are perfectionists sometimes push their children to eat healthy meals, cut out junk food, or participate in sports—not just within reason but to an extreme. Parents' overzealous demands can sometimes send the wrong message to their children. Instead of learning healthy behavior, the kids simply learn that their parents are not pleased with their appearance, which can damage self-esteem.

Researchers have long believed that certain personality characteristics may be passed on from parents to children. If this is so, as some evidence suggests, anorexia and bulimia may also be influenced by genetic makeup. Researchers are now studying the possibility that eating disorders might be hereditary. The best evidence for this theory comes from the study of twins. In observing identical twins, researchers have found that if one twin develops anorexia or bulimia, the second is at a much higher risk of having the same condition. Costin notes that "identical twins have a higher rate of shared eating disorder than do fraternal twins."[29] Though this provides evidence to support the genetic theory, other people argue that it can also support the theory that children simply model their parents' behavior. More research is needed to resolve this ongoing debate.

The Search for Biological Clues

Research into the possibility that heredity influences eating disorders has also spurred the search for a biological explanation for eating disorders, such as brain chemical disorders. According to Mary Ann Marrazzi, director of the Anorexia and Bulimia Research Center at Wayne State University in Detroit, "Anorexics and bulimics seem to have an inherited predisposition to a neurochemical disorder, like a predisposition to heart disease or cancer, except related to a family history of addiction and depression."[30] The key to determining if an eating disorder is hereditary, it seems, is to find a biological cause for the disorder and then track it from generation to generation. To date, biological research has uncovered a number of connections between eating disorders and how the brain functions or, more specifically, *mal*functions. These findings offer clues that the root of anorexia and bulimia might not just be a psychological problem, but a biological problem of the brain—one that may be passed on from parent to child.

Understanding hunger also helps in understanding eating disorders because hunger is actually triggered by a lack of blood

In searching for a biological explanation, researchers are exploring the possibility that the cause of eating disorders is passed from generation to generation within families.

sugar rather than just an empty stomach. Blood sugar levels are regulated by a section of the brain called the hypothalamus, which also regulates other vital functions such as body temperature, blood pressure, and heartbeat. When blood sugar falls below a certain level, the hypothalamus tells the body to eat and the hunger sensation switches on. However, the natural regulation of hunger that occurs in the brain can sometimes be impaired. This may occur for two reasons. First, experts have found that people whose brain chemistry does not function properly may develop symptoms of eating disorders. A second theory is that eating disorders are related to changes in the brain that occur specifically at puberty, which result in a hormonal imbalance.

Serotonin and Endorphins

Researchers have also identified two brain chemicals that may be linked to eating disorders, although it is difficult to determine if the elevated level of brain chemicals found in patients with eating disorders is the *cause* or the *effect* of the disorder. The brain chemical known as serotonin, for example, is currently being investigated.

Serotonin is a brain chemical that regulates mood and appetite. Recent research has shown that girls with eating disorders have higher than average levels of serotonin, which is thought to cause a loss of appetite. On the other hand, however, the body needs food in order to maintain normal serotonin levels. Without food the body's serotonin levels eventually fall, causing depression—another problem associated with anorexia.

Researchers have also found that emaciated anorexics have abnormally high brain levels of endorphins, similar to the elevated level of endorphins that can be produced in the brain by exercise such as running. Researchers theorize that starvation in anorexics produces a "high" like the kind runners say they experience. Doctors do not know, though, whether the endorphins are triggered by the lack of food or if the hypothalamus is actually malfunctioning. The malfunctioning hypothalamus, many doctors speculate, may be producing these endorphins and causing the anorexic to not want to eat, just as it is speculated that high levels of serotonin inhibit eating.

The brain chemical serotonin regulates mood and appetite and may be linked to eating disorders.

Hormonal Imbalances

Scientists are also studying hormonal imbalances that sometimes occur during puberty. Yet again, it is currently not clear whether these imbalances are the cause or the effect of the eating disorders. For example, many male anorexics have low levels of testosterone, a male hormone that stimulates male characteristics associated with puberty such as facial hair, change of voice, and sexual desire. Testosterone levels, though, are thought to improve in anorexic patients once they begin to gain weight. A boy who was treated for anorexia at age thirteen, for example, showed no interest in his peers, male or female, when he entered the program—a sign of low testosterone. As he gained weight, however, the boy became interested in his peers, and particularly in the females—a sign of restored testosterone.

Researchers also suspect that hormones might play a role in some females having an aversion to food. For example, researchers Carl and Joan Gustavson from Arizona State University at Tempe observed that some girls who experience a dramatic increase in concentrations of the female hormone estrogen during puberty develop an aversion to food. The Gustavsons speculated that these girls had abnormally low levels of estrogen before the onset of puberty. These low estrogen levels could best be compared to estrogen levels in males. The researchers speculated "that girls who produce low amounts of estrogen—possibly due to prenatal exposure to toxic substances—acquire a male-like estrogen sensitivity."[31]

To test their theory, the Gustavsons experimented with male rats and found that when the male rats were injected with increased levels of estrogen, they frequently became nauseated and developed taste aversions to food. The researchers believe, then, that when girls with malelike estrogen sensitivity stop eating, their estrogen level is reduced and the nauseating effect goes away.

Parental Influence Tied to Behavior

Though research into the possible hereditary influences of eating disorders has also spurred the search for a biological explanation for them, some scientists continue to explore the modeling theory. This is because many people—psychologists and the general population alike—hold parents accountable, in part, for children who later suffer from psychological problems. As a result there have been studies that focus on the relationship between patients who have eating disorders and each of their parents. These studies have tried to determine if one parent has more influence over a child than the other. However, researchers have found that the answer varies from girls to boys as well as from family to family.

As the primary caregiver, mothers were once thought to have more influence over their children. According to Denise Wilfley, codirector of the Yale University Center for Eating and Weight Disorders, "Studies have shown that mothers of anorexics tend to be excessively involved in their daughter's life, whereas mothers of bulimics tend to be very critical and uninvolved in their daughter's life."[32] In cases of anorexic males, studies have found mothers to be overinvolved and overprotective and sons to be very dependent on their mothers. Lack of assertiveness is a common

Parents' treatment of and influence over their children may have an affect on whether or not the child develops an eating disorder.

personality trait among anorexic males, and most psychologists believe this is due to this tendency to be dependent on others.

Fathers also can influence their children's attitudes toward food, their bodies, and themselves as much as mothers do. *Redbook* reported a study that supported this theory. It compared twenty-five women hospitalized for anorexia and bulimia against a control group that had no history of eating disorders. Researchers found little difference in each group's relationship with their mothers, but the relationship with the father was very different. According to journalist Judith Newman, "The women with eating disorders were far more likely to describe their fathers as critical and rejecting, and showed a lower level of attachment and satisfaction with the relationship."[33] In cases of anorexic males, studies have shown that their fathers were not very involved in the family.

Uniquely Human

Anorexia and bulimia will continue to be considered psychological "disorders" rather than medical "conditions" until biological research can offer conclusive evidence that eating disorders are caused by chemical or hormonal imbalances. Finding this evidence poses a great challenge to scientists because eating disorders are a uniquely human condition. They do not occur in other animals the way cancer, for example, can in dogs, mice, or rabbits. Scientists have learned much about cancer by studying its effects on animals and testing possible cures on them. With anorexia and bulimia, however, scientists must rely on studying people who suffer from these disorders and, more important, are willing to undergo treatment. The extent to which psychological, biological, and cultural factors—either individually or in combination—impact an individual seems to depend entirely upon the person's particular situation. So, until a definite cause and a definite cure are identified, treatments for anorexia and bulimia will continue to address primarily the possible psychological causes—problems that are unique to that individual and, above all, problems that may have nothing to do with food itself.

Chapter 3

Societal Pressures

M ANY PEOPLE BELIEVE that a teen's cultural environment plays a significant role in the development of eating disorders. This is because the cultural environment helps to shape a teen's attitudes toward the world and, above all, toward themselves. The cultural environment is broadly defined as anything that influences a teen outside of the family. It is the world of movies, fashion, music, television, and advertisements. Experts who study cultural influences on eating disorders are particularly interested in media messages about appearance. These messages generally define and often distort what it means to be beautiful.

This is especially true for females. Society and culture teaches females to associate their value with their appearance and bodies. Images from movies to television to advertising set a standard for beauty that women (and, increasingly, men also) often feel they should follow. Historian Joan Jacobs Brumberg of Cornell University, who studies eating disorders, believes that visual media such as television, films, videos, magazines, and particularly advertising "fuel the preoccupation with female thinness and serves as the primary stimulus for anorexia nervosa."[34]

Media Pressure to Be Thin

This image of the ideal female body has changed over time, just as the image of the ideal male body has changed more recently. During the 1950s, robust movie star Marilyn Monroe was the symbol of female beauty. However, over the past fifty years, as actresses have gotten thinner, so has society's idea of what makes a woman beautiful. Even Miss America finalists weigh less now than they did twenty years ago. In fact, being thin is considered one of today's chief attributes of beauty, particularly for females.

This idea is perpetuated by magazines, television, and even toy makers. Magazines directed at females, for example, are more

During the 1950s, Marilyn Monroe was society's idea of ideal female beauty.

likely than magazines directed at males to contain information about diets, suggestions on losing weight, and tips on clothes that will make readers look slimmer. Girls as young as twelve often feel pressured to conform to society's definition of beauty even though they may not realize it. Kelly Brownell, Ph.D., a professor of psychology at Yale University, explains that pre-teens are "bombarded by highly unrealistic ideals" and that a twelve-year-old "may not understand that the real body is different from the ideal body. It may seem that if you work hard enough, you can look just as you want to."[35] Toy companies also risk being accused of planting unrealistic ideals in young girls' minds with toys such as "Barbie," whose long legs, thin waist, and large breasts represent an idealized figure. In reality, female bodies come in all shapes and sizes, and rarely do these match the ideal.

Culture Defines Males, Too

Though males are traditionally more physically active than females and more concerned about growing or developing muscle rather than losing weight, they are increasingly becoming image-obsessed and self-critical. One reason is that teenage girls are no longer the exclusive target of the idealized body image perpetuated by culture and the media. More and more, males are being surrounded by images of thin, attractive, and successful role models in movies, television, music videos, and popular magazines. A *New York Times Magazine* style editor made the comment, "There's coming to be an acceptance of men as sex objects, men as beautiful."[36] The editor went on to point out that in addition to the latest fashions, male runway models sport flat, toned stomachs and that even men's department store mannequins are trim and muscular.

In 1993 a group of doctors surveyed men and women for *Psychology Today* to measure cultural changes in attitudes towards the male body. These doctors found that males believe their appearance is very important to women—more important even than the women who responded to the survey thought it was. Journalist Jill Neimark, whose article accompanied the survey,

Men are becoming increasingly critical of their appearance as they find themselves surrounded by media images of attractive, trim models.

reported that the rustic cowboy image that once stood for the standard of masculinity has been replaced by a highly muscular, powerfully shaped image—what Neimark refers to as hyper-masculine. She says, "It's an open question whether that standard will become as punishing for men as has the women's superthin standard."[37]

Culture Fuels Negative Self-Image

It is difficult to measure the influence that the media and society have on teens, but experts believe that the social and cultural pressure to conform to the media's idea of the perfect body creates a negative self-image that begins early. It makes children self-conscious about their appearance—a feeling that often begins at puberty.

Children generally start out liking their appearance, but learn to judge their own body against the idealized bodies they see in the media. Consequently, many children become displeased with their own appearance. For example, by asking children if they liked the way they looked in pictures, researchers at Connecticut College found that almost all first graders like their appearance. The number decreases to 77 percent in third graders, however, and to only 52 percent in fifth graders. Researchers believe that the results are linked not only to the media, but also to children becoming concerned with how their peers—particularly those of the opposite sex—perceive them. According to the lead researcher Joan Chrisler, Ph.D., "When kids get to the age where they think about what members of the opposite sex think of them, their self-esteem starts to go down."[38]

This is particularly true for girls. According to ANRED, more than half of teenage girls are, or think they should be, on diets. They want to lose all or some of the roughly forty pounds that females naturally gain during puberty, part of which is an increase in fat (particularly in the breasts and hips) that is necessary for the menstrual cycle. For girls, these physical changes—coupled with the cultural pressure to conform to society's accepted body image—create anxieties. Reporter Judith Newman discovered that "This terror of weight—the fear that one will grow into a teen, grow breasts and hips, and not stop growing—dominates the lives of many American girls."[39]

Just as puberty is a time of heightened anxiety for adolescent girls, it is especially frightening for athletes whose careers sometimes depend on maintaining a slim, boyish figure. Eighteen-year-old ice dancer Mica Darley, for instance, who was described

Societal Pressures

Girls are at high risk of developing an eating disorder during their teenage years when they begin to worry about what boys think of them.

as naturally thin, panicked when she turned fifteen. That's when the five-foot, four-inch, 107-pound athlete was confronted with what journalist Alison Bell refers to as one of the sport's biggest natural enemies: puberty. Bell writes, "Dismayed by her growing hips and breasts, she did what many top-level ice skaters and gymnasts do when their bodies begin to develop: deny it by going on a diet."[40]

Girls don't suffer from this terror in silence, however. They use it as an opportunity to bond with each other. Catherine Steiner-Adair, director of education, prevention, and outreach at the Harvard Eating Disorders Center, observed that beginning at about the age of ten or eleven, many preteen girls participate in "fat talk" in which they bond by talking about how much they hate their bodies. Steiner-Adair calls it a mutual body loathing and believes that girls participate in "fat talk" out of peer pressure. She says, "They think that if they don't participate in this conversation, they'll lose their friends."[41]

Early Maturers

Girls who mature early may be at a higher risk of developing anorexia or bulimia than girls who mature on time (typically between fourteen and eighteen years of age). In fact, a Columbia University study found that 3.5 percent of girls who developed early had eating disorders, while fewer than 1 percent of normal or late developers did. This is because girls who mature early tend to be highly self-conscious, even more so than the average teen. Julia A. Graber, Ph.D., associate director of the Adolescent Study Program at Columbia, says, "Early maturers tend to be more concerned with what boys find attractive than on-time girls, so they may begin to control their weight as a means of being more appealing."[42]

Boys Feel Pressure to Be Thin, Too

Regardless of when they mature, girls are typically more concerned about their appearance than boys are. However, boys are not immune to social pressures. Because males are increasingly being bombarded by images of the ideal male body in the media, they too fall prey to anxiety about weight and appearance, an anxiety that is similar to what most girls experience. Boys, however, have an added pressure: It is socially acceptable for girls to show concern about their appearance, but it is not acceptable for boys to do so. For example, boys don't typically engage in adolescent "fat talk." Instead, boys might talk about muscles and body strength. Or they may talk about exercising or dieting for their health. Both of these are socially acceptable ways of expressing their concerns about weight and appearance. These are also ways that boys conceal the insecurities they have developed because of pressure from the media and from their peers to have an ideal body.

Whereas females have a tendency to take dieting to an extreme, males have a tendency to take exercise to an extreme. One

Unlike young women, young men anxious about their weight and appearance generally exercise to excess rather than diet.

twelve-year-old boy, for example, was inspired by actor Sylvester Stallone's portrayal of "Rambo," a tough character with huge muscles who usually appeared shirtless. The boy started running eight to ten miles a day and eating nonfat foods. Experts not only fault the media for creating characters like Rambo, they also fault society for accepting—even admiring—exercise fanatics who try to look like Rambo. According to Steven Zelocoff, a Pittsburgh-based exercise physiologist, "You would be frowned upon for being neurotic about the way you eat, but celebrated as a local legend for the way you exercise."[43]

This extreme behavior, though, does not always have the desired effect. It can even have the opposite effect. For instance, the twelve-year-old's weight fell to 30 percent below normal, and instead of looking like his idol, he ended up looking frail.

Regardless, males who participate in these compulsive behaviors are classified as having an eating disorder. Even so, eating disorders are still commonly thought of as female illnesses, and those males who suffer from them often feel a sense of shame. They feel it is wrong to have developed a girl's illness. One junior high school football player and wrestler, who started bingeing and purging after his parents' divorce, recalls, "I felt like I was partaking in a woman's disease and that it wasn't very manly."[44] He reached the point where he was spending up to one hundred dollars on food and purging up to forty times—all in one day. Although he eventually sought help for his illness, many males are reluctant to enter treatment programs because they fear they might be the only male in a room filled with females.

Athletes Are Under Added Pressure

Athletes, in particular, are also influenced by images they see in the media—unrealistic ideas in the public's mind of what an athlete should look like. For example, the notions that gymnasts are supposed to be "tiny" and football players "huge" are perpetuated by society and the media. Experts believe these stereotypes make it easier for the athlete or coach to have unrealistic or unhealthy expectations of body size and shape: For an ice dancer, being ten pounds underweight is considered part of the job, and for ballet dancers it can be as much as twenty pounds. Mica, the ice dancer, summarized her job's demands in this way: "You are expected to have a model's body, but still be strong."[45]

This popular attitude, which is often called the "be thin to win" attitude, has become part of what some experts refer to as an "athletic culture," a group made up of athletes, coaches, and parents who are focused on appearance, weight, and performance. Many coaches monitor their athletes' weight through weekly weigh-ins. If an athlete's weight climbs above the accepted level, part of the coach's job is to see that he or she loses the unwanted pounds. A coach will also sometimes recommend that athletes lose weight if their performance is not up to the coach's expectations. Parents can also contribute to the problem, occasionally on the coach's orders. In turn, the athletes themselves develop unrealistic expectations regarding their weight and push themselves to extremes, sometimes to the point of injury. Too much exercise and not enough food can lead to grumpiness, mental dullness, lack of energy, difficulty completing workouts, and slower times in clocked events—the exact opposite of what the athlete is trying to achieve.

In addition to the pressure of competition, athletes feel added pressure because their bodies are constantly on display. The uniforms of many sports, such as leotards for dancing and gymnastics or spandex tops and shorts for runners or bikers, are formfitting. One female swimmer who battled bulimia for ten years finally stopped competing because she couldn't bear to wear a swimsuit anymore. She felt it exposed too much of her body.

United States, Europe, and Japan Top the List

Although the pressure on females, males, and athletes to be thin can be great, it is a phenomenon that exists only in a few cultures. According to Margo Maine, Ph.D., director of eating disorders at the Institute of Living in Hartford, Connecticut, "There is a huge cultural preoccupation in the United States, with body weight, size and appearance."[46] That preoccupation, though, is not confined to the United States. It also occurs in Europe, Japan, and other industrialized nations. Experts believe the reason is that teens in these areas are equally influenced by fashion, movies, music, and sports.

Conversely, anorexia and bulimia are not a problem in other parts of the world. People who live in remote areas of Mexico or

Eating disorders are most common in industrial nations like the United States where people are influenced by fashion, movies, and music.

Africa, for example, are not at risk for developing eating disorders because teens in those regions are not exposed to popular culture. Also, in some of these areas, people do not have access to the wide variety and abundance of food available in most highly modern societies. When food is scarce, it is unlikely that people will choose not to eat what they do have as with anorexia, or to binge and purge as with bulimia.

However, teens from low-risk areas can develop eating disorders if they move to high-risk areas like the United States, Japan, or Europe. Researchers have looked at recent immigrants to the United States, for example, and discovered that they sometimes develop anorexia and bulimia as they try to adjust to the American lifestyle and its cultural preoccupation with being thin.

In some instances, American cultural attitudes also have found their way into low-risk and remote areas. When satellite TV became available in remote parts of the South Pacific, for example, an interesting phenomenon occurred. There, particularly in Fiji, people love food, and their idea of the perfect body is bigger than the American ideal. However, when Fijian teens started to watch the skinny actresses in shows like *Melrose Place* and *Beverly Hills 90210,* the girls wanted to be thinner. A *Newsweek* reporter observed, "Now Fijian teenage girls are not only adopting the clothing and hairstyles of Western women, some are showing serious symptoms of eating disorders."[47] In fact, the more TV the Fijian girls watched, the fatter they felt.

Excessive TV Watching

In addition to making teens feel fat, excessive television watching can actually cause them to become fat due to inactivity. Some experts say that teens spend an average of twenty-two hours a week watching television rather than being active. So, though they may want to look like the skinny actresses and models they see on television, they end up with a body that is far from this ideal. In addition, teens who are inactive have fewer opportunities to socialize with peers, which may lead to low self-esteem—a risk factor for developing an eating disorder. Therefore, anxiety about weight and personal appearance may be heightened even further in teens who gain weight due to a sedentary lifestyle.

Watching too much TV is also thought to influence teens' attitudes towards food. In particular, teens may desire unhealthy food because television commercials tend to showcase unhealthy food.

Excessive television watching can lead to inactivity, weight gain, and eating disorders.

In an article on childhood obesity, Beatrice Trum Hunter writes, "By adolescence, a child has watched 15,000 hours of television, and has been exposed to 350,000 commercials, more than half of which promote highly processed food products and soft drinks."[48] Hunter also reports that childhood obesity is often followed by efforts to control the child's diet, which can sometimes lead to eating disorders. Thus, the struggle between wanting to look model-thin and wanting to eat unhealthy food may lead to bulimia. Adolescents and teens who cannot control their cravings may decide to eat all they want, and then purge to maintain or lose weight. In the process they damage their bodies.

Findings such as these lead experts to believe that the media plays a significant role in influencing teen behavior, including behavior that can lead to anorexia and bulimia. However, it is difficult for those experts to determine the extent of the media's role. Regardless, researchers know that the media, combined with peer pressure and societal attitudes, contribute to the development of eating disorders. Moreover, they know that these factors do not influence only females, as was previously thought; these factors affect males as well as specific populations, such as athletes or teens from industrialized nations. As experts continue their search for the exact causes of anorexia and bulimia, media influences and societal pressures also will continue to be scrutinized as potential causes of these conditions.

Chapter 4

The Dangers of Eating Disorders

A NOREXIA AND BULIMIA are dangerous illnesses that can lead to serious physical damage and even death. However, many teens who develop anorexia and bulimia are often not aware of the dangers their illnesses present. These teens believe that they have found a simple solution to losing weight. They usually see immediate—sometimes dramatic—results, and are encouraged by those results. Further, they also like the compliments they receive from family and friends about their new and improved appearance. However, as the teen's illness progresses, family and friends might begin to express concern, asking questions such as "Don't you think you are too thin?" But these questions do not cause the teen to be alarmed. In fact, the opposite occurs. Anorexics and bulimics are usually pleased to hear these questions, which they perceive as more compliments. Some anorexics and bulimics even mistake the concern of family and friends for jealousy.

Even though anorexics and bulimics usually enjoy the attention they receive when they begin to lose weight, they generally do not show off their thin bodies. In fact, they usually hide their frail figures with clothing. Some even wear large or baggy clothing to further disguise their illness. This way, anorexics and bulimics may continue to lead normal lives while keeping their illness a secret.

Further, because the damaging physical effects of anorexia and bulimia may not be immediately felt, the dangers are not immediately apparent. Many anorexics and bulimics suffer for months and sometimes even years before complications arise and they are forced to seek medical treatment. In terms of anorexia, *Time* magazine reports that "most deaths from the condition occur in women over 45."[49] This is likely because they refused treatment or denied their illness for such a long period of time, their bodies were no longer able to function. Even so, younger anorexics also risk death as well as permanent injury.

The Physical Effects of Anorexia

Although people with eating disorders can succeed in fooling their family, their friends, and even themselves into thinking they are perfectly healthy, their bodies become weak. In this weakened condition, maintaining a normal lifestyle becomes impossible. Even though some anorexics appear to be very active, sometimes exercising vigorously as a means of distraction and as a way to lose even more weight, most don't have much energy, a sign that the body is missing proper nutrients. The problem is further compounded in anorexics in particular by the fact that many suffer from sleeplessness which results in exhaustion and an inability to concentrate.

These factors often result in anorexics or bulimics, former overachievers with great grades, finding it hard to keep up with the demands of school. Often, their grades begin to suffer, and anorexics in particular have been known to pass out in the classroom. One anorexic girl went out for a walk and never came home. Her mother found her a few blocks away, collapsed on the sidewalk, and had to carry her home.

While students with anorexia perform poorly in the classroom, athletes with anorexia perform poorly in competition. Poor nutrition leaves them vulnerable to sickness (due to a weakened immune system) and injury. It also takes much longer to recover from an injury.

As anorexics, athlete or not, lose more and more weight, they begin to develop symptoms of starvation, including a skeletal appearance, thinning hair, hair loss, dry or yellow-tinged skin, sunken eyes, and brittle nails. After Martha took a shower, for

Warning Signs of Anorexia

▶ Significant weight loss

▶ Continuing to diet (although thin)

▶ Distorted body image (feeling fat even when thin)

▶ Fear of weight gain

▶ In females, lack of menstrual periods

▶ Preoccupation with food, calories, nutrition, and/or cooking

▶ Preferring to exercise alone

▶ Compulsive exercising

▶ Bingeing and purging

Source: The American Anorexia/Bulimia Association, Inc.

example, she noticed that the drain would be full of hair. She also noticed that her fingernails had turned purple, another sign of starvation and one she attempted to hide. She recalls, "My nails were purplish. Everyone noticed that, so I started wearing nail polish."[50]

Other, less visible, symptoms of starvation include the body losing its ability to produce heat and process food. Many anorexics report that they feel cold all the time. Martha remembers that the only time she actually felt warm was in the bathtub. Some anorexics also notice that fine, downy hair known as lanugo begins to appear on their face, back, and arms. This is the body's attempt to defend itself against the cold—a visible sign of anorexia. And they may experience digestive problems. Further, an anorexic who begins to eat normally again may experience abdominal pain or constipation because the body is not used to processing food.

Amenorrhea

In females, anorexia results in additional internal problems. The disorders can affect the menstrual cycle and possibly result in infertility. For example, anorexia has been linked to a condition known as amenorrhea (absence of the menstrual cycle). An anorexic might find that her monthly periods stop (secondary amenorrhea) or, if she develops anorexia in puberty, that they never begin at all (primary amenorrhea). Typically amenorrhea is caused by pregnancy, an ovulation abnormality, a birth defect, or a thyroid disorder. Amenorrhea can also occur in the obese, due to excess fat cells interfering with the process of ovulation. However, in anorexics, amenorrhea occurs because the reproductive system just shuts down due to malnourishment. This is a result of not maintaining a body weight high enough to sustain a pregnancy. Women athletes sometimes experience amenorrhea due to low body fat as well.

Complications can arise in women who have missed two or more consecutive periods. This is because the uterus does not expel its nonfertilized egg and endometrium lining—a process that would normally occur on a monthly basis. According to the Methodist Health Care System's website, "Without this monthly expulsion, the risk of uterine cancer increases."[51]

Amenorrhea has also been linked to osteoporosis, a condition that anorexics run the risk of developing. "Osteoporosis" is a bone disease that translates to "porous bones." People with osteoporosis suffer from a lack of bone mass, meaning their bones are weak and brittle compared to a healthy person's, whose bones are strong and dense. A person's bones continually undergo what experts refer to as a remodeling process in which they are constantly being broken down and built up. Early in life the buildup is greater than the breakdown, and females reach peak bone density at about age fifteen, after which it increases slightly until the mid-thirties and then declines until the breakdown eventually outpaces the buildup. This is why osteoporosis typically occurs in women over sixty and can cause complications such as hip fractures.

The Physical Dangers of Anorexia

▶ Irregular heartbeat

▶ In females, lack of menstrual periods

▶ Dehydration, kidney stones, or kidney failure

▶ Lanugo, or fine body hair that develops to keep body warm

▶ Muscle atrophy

▶ Bowel irritation and constipation

▶ Osteoporosis as a result of calcium loss

Source: National Eating Disorders Organization.

However, it can affect women of all ages. For example, studies of female athletes who suffer from amenorrhea have shown that they have significant losses in bone density. According to a leading researcher on amenorrhea-related bone loss, "Some amenorrheic female athletes in their 20s have the same bone density as women in their 70s and 80s."[52] Because osteoporosis causes bones to fracture or break, athletes with amenorrhea are at greater risk for injury. Even nonathletic women who have anorexia-induced amenorrhea can experience stress fractures just from walking. According to Carolyn Costin, it is not known if this loss of bone density is reversible.

Other Internal Problems

Just as starvation can weaken bones, it can also weaken organs. For example, severe weight loss causes heart muscle fibers to thin, resulting in a slowed heart rate, low blood pressure, and occasionally heart valve abnormalities which can lead to palpitations, chest pain, and arrhythmia (an irregular heartbeat). A heartbeat that's too fast (rapid arrhythmia) can cause a heart attack, and a heartbeat that's too slow (slow arrhythmia) can trigger fainting and injury from a resulting fall.

Anorexia also significantly strains the kidneys, liver, and other internal organs. For example, an Olympic hopeful, gymnast Christy Henrich, slipped into a coma and died in 1994 of multiple organ failure. According to one report, Christy went in and out of fifteen hospitals and, at one point, got down to a frightening forty-two pounds. She died at the age of twenty-two, weighing only sixty-one pounds at four feet and one inch tall.

The gastrointestinal tract is also affected by severe weight loss. This is because the rate that the body processes food out of the stomach and through the digestive tract is significantly slowed. This is not necessarily a problem when the patient is suffering from anorexia, but it can lead to problems when the patient is recovering. An anorexic who begins to eat again will

Anorexics run the risk of developing osteoporosis, a bone disease which usually affects women over sixty years old.

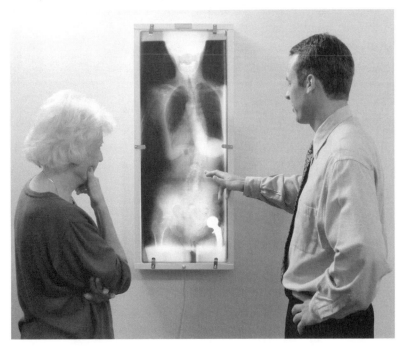

Gymnast Christy Henrich (pictured in 1993) died in August 1994 of multiple organ failure caused by anorexia; she weighed only sixty-one pounds when she died.

feel full immediately due to the body's slow rate of digestion. Recovering anorexics, for instance, may complain of abdominal pain and constipation because it might take three to six days for food to pass through the digestive system before it returns to normal.

The Physical Effects of Bulimia

Bulimics are more able than anorexics to continue to lead a normal lifestyle even while they suffer from the disorder because the physical effects of bulimia are not as drastic. Bulimics do not experience the anorexic's severe weight loss, so they don't have the symptoms affiliated with starvation. No one has been known to die from bulimia. However, there are physical effects that are unique to bulimia, mostly related to the constant purging of food, which can result in serious injuries.

As with anorexia, some of the physical effects of bulimia are visible. One early complication of self-induced vomiting—and the most visible sign of bulimia—is parotid gland enlargement, which results in a noticeable swelling between the jawbone and the neck and, in severe cases, can look like what Carolyn Costin refers to as a chipmunk-type faces. Also, due to the presence of stomach acid in vomit, bulimia causes dental problems, including an increase in cavities, inflamed gums, and other periodontal diseases. Erosion of tooth enamel, however, is probably the most common dental complication of bulimia. It usually occurs in the area of the teeth closest to the tongue. Costin writes, "Patients who induce vomiting at a minimum frequency of three times per week for a year will show erosion of tooth enamel."[53] This can lead to a sensitivity to hot and cold foods. Vomiting may also cause broken blood vessels in the eyes as well as cracked and dry lips.

In addition, self-induced vomiting can cause serious internal damage. For example, just as stomach acid can erode tooth enamel, it can also irritate the esophagus. Thus, bulimics sometimes develop a condition known as esophagitis in which they experience heartburn pain due to a damaged esophagus lining. Costin further reports that repeated vomiting can actually tear the lining of the esophagus and cause a bulimic to vomit blood. The esophagus can also rupture completely, resulting in severe chest pain. Bulimics also run the risk of developing cardiac arrhythmia, seizures, muscle spasms, and cancer. Costin says, "Repeated exposure of the esophageal lining to the acidic stomach contents can result in the development of a precancerous lesion referred to as Barrett's esophagus."[54]

Bulimics who rely on laxatives to eliminate food from their bodies also suffer from electrolyte imbalances as well as colon damage. Overuse of laxatives can injure the colonic neurons which control the contractions that push waste out of the body, resulting in a condition known as cathartic colon syndrome in which patients have problems controlling their bowels, suffer from constipation, or experience abdominal discomfort. Damage to the colon can be permanent, and surgery may be necessary to correct this problem. Laxative abusers must be identified early, before colon damage occurs. They will experience bloating and must eat a high-fiber diet, drink abundant fluids, and exercise. Still, it may take weeks to restore normal colon function, which makes laxative withdrawal more difficult than stopping vomiting.

Getting Out of Control

Though the symptoms of self-induced vomiting can be treated with medications to lessen their effects, the only way to reverse the physical damage of self-induced vomiting is to stop doing it. In some cases, however, what began as a voluntary behavior—vomiting that the teen could control—can become an involuntary

Many bulimics use over-the-counter laxatives to help eliminate food from their bodies; overuse of these products, though, can cause permanent damage.

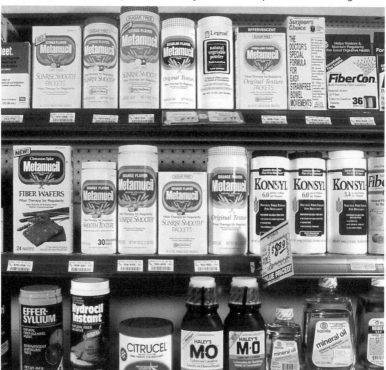

Bulimics soon discover that purging after a binge becomes involuntary. Their bodies become conditioned to vomit in response to eating.

behavior. For example, bulimics who constantly force themselves to throw up after eating might find that vomiting becomes automatic. It turns into an involuntary, uncontrollable response to eating food. Carolyn Costin reports that some patients experience spontaneous vomiting (sometimes referred to as esophageal reflux) or severe indigestion in which food comes back up into the mouth with no forced effort on the patient's part.

Depression

In addition to the many physical problems associated with eating disorders, anorexics and bulimics suffer from serious psychological problems. The most common is depression. Depression can describe a normal human emotion, but it can also refer to a psychological illness. Depression tends to run in families, meaning teens who have depressed parents are often depressed themselves. However, outside factors can also trigger depression. In fact, some factors that are thought to trigger eating disorders, such as low self-esteem, abuse, or the emotional stress of divorce, changing schools, or moving, are also thought to trigger depression.

Experts have noted a high rate of depression among patients with eating disorders, but they do not know if depression causes the eating disorder or if the eating disorder causes depression. Depression affects about 5 percent of teens and adolescents and, according to the Focus Adolescent Services website, seems to be on the rise. The website states, "Over the past 50 years, depression has become more common and is now recognized at increasingly younger ages."[55] Signs of serious depression include frequent sadness, crying for no apparent reason, a sense of hopelessness, a loss of interest in activities, low energy, boredom, anger, hostility, inability to concentrate, poor performance in school, thoughts of suicide, and self-destructive behavior. Loss of appetite often accompanies depression, as well, and can lead to anorexia or bulimia.

The most acute danger of depression is that it can lead to suicide. In fact, people with anorexia are thought by experts to be at a higher risk than the general population for suicide resulting from depression. According to the American Psychiatric Association, between 2 and 5 percent of the 10 percent of anorexics who die from the illness commit suicide. Carolyn Costin reports that bulimia has also been linked with mood disorders, particularly depression. She notes, "Some researchers reported that as many as 80 percent of bulimic patients studied had major mood disorders at some point during their lives."[56] Even so, bulimics do not seem to be at risk for suicide. This is probably due to the fact that bulimics tend to respond better than anorexics to treatment for depression.

Low Weight over Good Health

The effects of anorexia and bulimia vary greatly from case to case. While a bone density test might indicate a severe loss in one anorexic, it may show none in another. Further, many symptoms of eating disorders—headaches, stomachaches, and fainting spells, for example—do not show up in test results.

And, just as anorexics and bulimics are encouraged by concerned comments about their weight to continue to starve or vomit, they are often not deterred by medical consequences. Costin says that some feel it is more important to be thin than to be healthy. Moreover, those who receive normal lab results in the early stages of anorexia and bulimia may believe that, because their illness has not yet hurt them, they can continue to undereat or binge and purge without any consequences. The reality, though, is that no one is immune to the long-term effects of anorexia and bulimia.

Chapter 5

Treatment and Recovery

EXPERTS OFTEN LIKEN anorexia and bulimia to other addictive behaviors such as smoking, drug abuse, and alcoholism. In these cases of addiction, the solution is to take away the problem—cigarettes, drugs, or alcohol. Yet, in treating an eating disorder, the problem is food, something the body needs to survive. Thus, instead of abstaining from the source of their problem, which is the typical approach to controlling addictive behavior, anorexics and bulimics must develop healthy eating habits, which means changing their destructive habits and learning to deal properly with food.

Treatment Is Difficult

Eating disorders are complex to treat because they combine psychological, cultural, and biological factors. Even though research into the biological causes of eating disorders continues to offer new forms of medical treatment for anorexia and bulimia, the traditional method of treatment is still psychological counseling or therapy. The goal of therapy is to change the anorexic's or bulimic's behavior as well as the person's attitude toward food. Therapy is considered a long-term treatment, one that may take months or even years to be fully effective.

Problems arise, though, because the physical effects of anorexia and bulimia often require medical treatment. Although medication and surgery can lessen or repair the damage anorexia and bulimia do to the body, these solutions are short-term and not considered sufficient treatments. This is because providing

Treatment and Recovery

the body with proper nutrition is the best defense against the injurious physical effects of anorexia and bulimia, and it is also the first step in the recovery process. Establishing healthy eating habits is the key to this step. Thus, for anorexics, this first step means learning to eat again. For bulimics, it means no longer purging.

Family Versus Hospital Care

In the early stages of anorexia and bulimia, before the physical effects begin to damage the body, family and friends often initiate the recovery process by showing concern and offering support. Parents often provide the added attention and special support teens need in order for them to take this first step. One mother remembers driving from store to store as her daughter

Family and friends usually initiate the recovery process for a person suffering from anorexia or bulmia.

searched for the "perfect" banana. Dr. B. Timothy Walsh commended that mother, who eventually helped her daughter recover from anorexia. He said, "She [the mother] learned that there is no substitute for spending long and difficult hours with patients, whose ideas about what and how much they should eat are remarkably irrational."[57]

When patients do not respond to family support or when they begin to suffer from the physical effects of anorexia and bulimia, they may need to be placed in a controlled environment. This is especially true in the later stages of anorexia and bulimia, when the physical effects can become life-threatening. This usually means an extended hospital stay where patients are generally given four to six closely supervised meals a day, with specific mealtime goals and specific consequences for not meeting those goals. As Lisa Jennifer Selzman, an eating-disorder therapist, explains, "One person's goal might be to add two scary foods (a tablespoon of mayonnaise; a pancake) back into her diet; another's might be that if she doesn't eat three quarters of her meal, she'll have to drink a liquid supplement."[58]

The goal of both family support and hospital care is to help patients begin to eat (or, in the case of bulimics, to fully digest what they eat) on their own. However, patients sometimes are physically not able to do this. Anorexics, for example, might be so weak from starvation that they are unable to eat on their own. Or a bulimic might have damage to the esophagus, or may have reached the point where vomiting has become an involuntary reaction to food. In these instances, or when a life is in immediate danger, patients need to be forced to eat in order for their bodies to receive nutrients. In such cases doctors may need to pump fluids into the patient intravenously, or send nutrients through a tube that runs from the patient's nose directly to the stomach.

Weight Stabilization

In addition to closely monitoring the patient's meals, the medical staff also monitors the patient's health. This is because gaining weight can strain the body, just as losing weight can. According to doctors, "Gaining more than three or four pounds a week carries the physical risk of heart failure and systemic shock because organs that have been starved cannot keep up with the increased body mass."[59] As a result, doctors and nurses closely observe a patient's vital signs to avoid complications and ensure that weight gain occurs at a safe pace.

Safe and stable weight gain is an important factor in recovery. *Good Housekeeping* reported that, in a study of twenty-three hospitalized anorexics at the University of Pittsburgh, more than half who were discharged while still underweight (after about three to seven weeks of treatment) required rehospitalization, whereas only 15 percent who left after they'd gained adequate weight (after about two to six months) required readmittance.

People suffering from anorexia or bulimia need to be hospitalized if the effects of the disorders become life threatening.

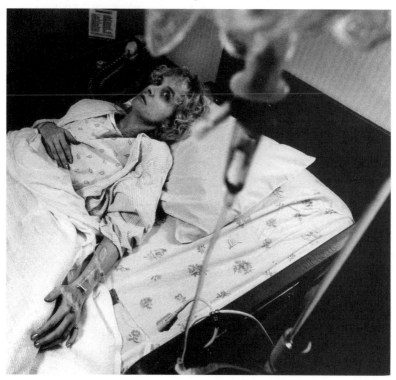

Roadblocks to Recovery

However, there are a number of obstacles to recovery. Patients who are unable or unwilling to eat, for example, must become comfortable again with the motions of eating. Something as easy as chewing and swallowing, simple tasks that most people do without thinking, are exceedingly difficult for anorexics. They also have a hard time accepting the feeling of fullness that follows a meal. Selzman says, "The aim is to make eating feel *normal* again."[60]

To correct these destructive habits, treatment must go beyond diet alone. In addition to supervising meals, medical staff must monitor the patients' behavior to ensure that they are not only eating, but fully digesting their meals. In cases of bulimia, bathroom privileges might be restricted to ensure that patients don't vomit after meals. Patients who purge through other methods must also be monitored. One patient, for example, was not allowed to leave the facility for the privilege of a ten-minute walk after it was discovered that she had gone to the hospital pharmacy to buy a box of laxatives. Another patient continued to lose weight even though she was observed eating her meals. She was discovered secretly exercising in her room for hours, both morning and night. And gymnast Christy Henrich had to be confined to a wheelchair during her treatment for anorexia to prevent her from running everywhere in an attempt to lose weight.

Another obstacle is that patients often resist doctors' attempts to feed them. Eating makes them feel fat. Thus, even in closely monitored settings, anorexics and bulimics find ways to fool the doctors and nurses. They might hide their food under a mattress, for instance, or vomit and then drink gallons of water before their scheduled weigh-ins. In response, doctors and nurses sometimes use their own tricks to help patients recover. For example, a patient might be required to step on the scale, but facing away from the number. In such cases they are told only whether they gained or lost weight, not the actual number of pounds. Many doctors have found that this method helps reduce the patient's anxiety about gaining weight.

Cost Concerns

Another obstacle to recovery is cost. Patients are sometimes discharged early due to the cost of treatment, and early discharge can lead to a relapse. A person suffering from anorexia might require up to three months of intensive hospitalization as well as years of outpatient treatment to prevent a relapse, at a cost of upwards of $150,000 according to some experts. In the case of Maura Kelly, a recovering anorexic who started dieting at age twelve, recovery took much longer. She says, "It took a grand total of 11 years, more than 120 days in the hospital, some 1,500 hours of therapy, innumerable hours scribbling in my journal and $250,000 of my dad's money—insurance only covered about $20,000—to finally get free of my anorexia."[61]

Many people are not able to cover these enormous costs personally and must rely solely on insurance. However, because insurance companies still consider anorexia and bulimia to be psychiatric disorders, insurers do not generally cover medical benefits for patients who suffer from these illnesses. Although some insurers do cover psychiatric treatment, the number of therapy sessions are limited and, again, are usually not enough to get the illness completely under control. Vivian Hanson Meehan, president and founder of the National Association of Anorexia Nervosa and Associated Disorders (ANAD), says, "A lot of people who need treatment today are not getting it, and the people who are getting treatment are getting inadequate treatment because of their insurance companies."[62] Insurers do cover hospital stays for anorexics and bulimics whose lives are in immediate danger due to the physical effects of these illnesses. However, the patients are discharged as soon as the particular physical problem is under control, whether or not the causes of the anorexia or bulimia are under control.

Treating Athletes

Treating athletes who suffer from anorexia and bulimia poses another special problem for therapists, especially for those who might not be familiar with an athlete's demanding routine. According to Katherine Fulkerson, Ph.D., what might be a perfectly reasonable exercise regimen for an athlete might seem extreme to an ordinary therapist. Fulkerson says, "The therapist hears that this woman [an athlete] is exercising two hours a day, and to him it's off the end of the spectrum."[63] Experts are therefore calling for a unique set of guidelines to treat anorexia and bulimia among athletes.

In order to create new treatment guidelines, however, doctors must first develop a new way to define eating disorders among

Treating athletes who have eating disorders is particularly challenging since their lifestyles are so different from non-athletes.

athletes that take into account the athlete's unique lifestyle. For example, standard tests for diagnosing eating disorders typically rely strictly on body weight. However, what's considered a normal weight for the average person might be considered high for an athlete. According to Fulkerson, the main concern is the athlete's health—both physical and mental. She believes, "When exercise and eating cease to be goal driven and the point is just to be thinner, when the focus is on how much you're eating and how much you need to exercise to get it off, then the activity has gone past being an athletic endeavor and instead becomes part of an eating disorder."[64]

Experts, including Fulkerson, agree that because coaches are such powerful influences in the lives of athletes, they must be involved in the treatment and recovery process. This means that coaches must be aware of weight goals and limits on physical activity that doctors may have outlined for their patients. Ideally, coaches will become part of what some experts refer to as a treatment team that typically includes a doctor who monitors and treats physical problems, a therapist who uncovers and treats psychological causes, and a dietitian who provides nutritional counseling.

Behavioral Therapy Is Key to Recovery

Although weight stabilization is the first step in the recovery process, just because a patient begins to eat and gain weight doesn't mean that a full recovery has been achieved. In fact, there is an ongoing debate about how to define recovery. The medical definition of an anorexic is one who refuses to maintain their weight above the lowest weight considered normal for the person's age and height, and one whose total body weight is at least 15 percent below normal. Researchers have found, though, that reaching normal weight does not necessarily constitute recovery. Kathrine Halmi, M.D., of Cornell Medical Center, insists, "Recovery also means no longer expressing a fear of getting fat or being obsessively preoccupied with weight, and eating normally."[65] As a result, simply eating again isn't enough. People with anorexia and bulimia, whether in the early or latter stages,

Recovery from an eating disorder must include professional counseling; otherwise the patient is likely to return to destructive habits.

generally need professional counseling to change their actions and attitudes about food.

The most common form of counseling for anorexia and bulimia is cognitive-behavioral therapy, which focuses directly on the disorder's symptoms. The goal is to change poor eating habits by correcting the patient's negative attitudes about food and body shape. To do this, counselors may give patients "homework," such as keeping a journal of what they eat, when they eat, and how they feel when they eat. Other assignments might include eating a certain number of meals at specific intervals each day. These methods are designed to establish normal and consistent eating patterns. For example, one patient was instructed to eat dinner at a specific time each evening instead of eating just when she felt hungry. By learning to shop for groceries and plan her meals in advance, she was able to stop rushing out to grab anything she could find to eat when hunger struck. Other patients need to learn to eat all meals—even a snack of cookies—in normal portions from a plate while sitting at a table rather than in handfuls out of a box while standing in the kitchen.

Sometimes when patients are asked to record how they feel when they eat, as in journal writing, strong emotions surface that patients are often not prepared to deal with. In some cases anorexics and bulimics have starved or purged for years to avoid facing these emotions, because confronting them is sometimes even more scary than confronting their illness. The discovery of these hidden emotions adds to the patient's existing stress, which includes anger at being forced to eat and fear of becoming fat. Many patients experience irritability or depression as a result. Martha, for example, admitted herself to an eating disorder program and underwent therapy when she was diagnosed with anorexia. The reporter who interviewed her family found that, "When her family visited, they often found Martha cranky or depressed from the strain of all the therapy, new emotions, and unwanted food."[66]

Confronting Buried Emotions

While cognitive-behavior therapy addresses the disorder itself, other therapies address the emotions that are thought to be the underlying cause of the disorder. One treatment, interpersonal therapy (IPT), was originally developed to treat depression and has recently been adapted for treating bulimia. It is based on the notion that people with eating disorders often use food as a substitute for emotions or feelings. Some patients are aware of

Treatment

Treatment for people with eating disorders may include:

Hospitalization	to prevent death, suicide, and medical crisis
Medication	to relieve depression and anxiety
Dental work	to repair damage and minimize future problems
Individual counseling	to develop healthy ways of taking control
Group counseling	to learn how to manage relationships effectively
Family counseling	to change old patterns and create healthier new ones
Nutrition counseling	to debunk food myths and design healthy meals
Support groups	to break down isolation and alienation

Source: Anorexia Nervosa and Related Eating Disorders, Inc.

this connection and others are not. A boy whose parents separated when he was nine, for example, admitted that his obsessing over food was the only way to alleviate his depression. In therapy, Lauren M. Frasciello, M.D., and Susan G. Willard, M.S.W., reported that "he was able to retrieve memories of the unsettling and sad feelings he had had around his parents' bad relationship and eventual divorce."[67] The therapist helped him to understand the feelings he had toward his mother, father, and stepfather. Later he learned to express those feelings in family therapy sessions. In this case the individual therapist and the family therapist worked together to help the boy fully recover.

Some patients, though, do not realize immediately that their eating disorder is indirectly connected to emotions. One woman with bulimia for instance, through IPT, discovered that she was suffering from sadness over her sister's death and from loneliness over her recent divorce. With IPT, the woman was able to work through those emotions and as a result overcome her bulimia.

Because IPT does not directly address the patient's behavior toward food, it is considered an *indirect* method of treating an eating disorder. Therefore, a patient in IPT may take longer to recover from an eating disorder than a patient in cognitive-behavioral therapy. However, many doctors believe that this recovery will be longer lasting than one from cognitive-behavioral therapy because the underlying causes of the eating disorder will have been revealed and worked out.

Positive and Realistic Thinking

Another method therapists sometimes use to separate food from emotions involves positive and realistic thinking. Many eating-disorder patients who are in reality too thin believe they are too fat. Their attitudes are negative. For example, an anorexic might claim she is disgusted by her fat arms or thighs.

To combat this unrealistic and negative thinking, Lisa Jennifer Selzman, an eating disorder therapist, asks her patients to look at their reflection in a mirror—something that is truly painful for most of them to do—and describe what they see. Selzman found that patients tended to describe their appearance in terms of feelings. So when her patients claim that they feel fat, she explains that fat is not a feeling. She asks them to replace the word fat with a word that describes what the patient is actually feeling—anger, sadness, or fear, for instance. In this way patients eventually learn to accept their bodies and uncover their hidden feelings. Selzman says, "My job is to take the focus off body size and concentrate on the patient's emotional life instead."[68] She also tries to get her patients to focus on what they like about their appearance instead of what they don't like.

Treating Anorexia and Bulimia with Medication

Though therapy is the most common approach to treating anorexia and bulimia, medication is sometimes used in conjunction with therapy. However, medication alone is not used as a treatment for eating disorders. The reason is that patients must change their eating habits as well as their negative attitudes about food and how it affects their appearance. This can be achieved only through therapy. Medication can sometimes be useful, however, when a patient does not immediately respond to therapy due, for example, to depression or because of a brain chemical imbalance.

Therapist Lisa Jennifer Selzman has her patients look in a mirror and describe what they see. This exercise helps them separate their appearance from their feelings.

Treatment and Recovery

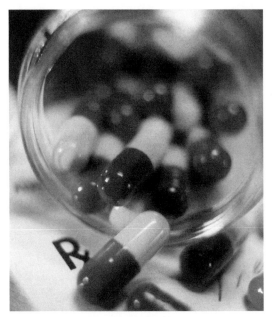

Studies show that anorexics and bulimics respond well to antidepressant medications.

Antidepressants are the most commonly prescribed types of medication for eating disorder patients. Studies have shown that both bulimics and anorexics respond well to antidepressants. In bulimics, studies show that antidepressants reduce binge eating and purging. In anorexics, imbalances in the brain chemical serotonin can be stabilized through the use of antidepressants.

The use of medication to treat anorexia and bulimia is not limited to antidepressants, however. One group of doctors, for example, was successful in treating anorexics and bulimics through a combination of therapy and Naltrexone, a drug typically used to cure heroin addicts. What prompted these doctors to try Naltrexone was the theory that eating disorders are caused by malfunctioning chemical signals in the brain or by a genetic predisposition. This theory has led some doctors to claim that anorexics are actually addicted to starvation or, specifically, that they are addicted to the release of brain chemicals caused by starvation. The doctors theorize that the addiction manifests itself in bulimics as a need to binge, which is a response to the release of brain chemicals that signal starvation. With Naltrexone, the patients were able to resume eating to the point where the body was no longer sensing starvation and the brain was no longer producing a chemical reaction in response to starvation. At that point patients were able to undergo therapy in order to correct their poor eating habits and negative attitudes toward food—information that the brain was previously unable to process because of the starvation-induced chemical imbalance.

Although certain medications have proven helpful in treating anorexia and bulimia in combination with therapy, scientists are still searching for a medication to exclusively treat, and ideally cure, eating disorders. Biological research, which continues to shed new light on the possible causes of anorexia and bulimia, seems to hold the key. Marsha Marcus, psychologist and chief of the Eating Disorders Department at the University of Pittsburgh School of Medicine, says, "Conditions like anorexia and bulimia are probably triggered and maintained by psychological and cultural factors, but if we can identify a biological component, there might be medicines we can develop to control it."[69]

Outlook for Recovery

Recovery from anorexia is possible, however only one-third of patients can expect to be completely cured. *Good Housekeeping* reports that "With counseling and medication, about one third are cured. Another third improve but never fully recover, and the rest wage a lifelong battle."[70] Dr. Walsh reports that 20 to 30 percent of anorexic patients remain chronically ill, no matter what treatment they receive. However, experts believe that anorexics who seek treatment in the early stages of the illness have a greater chance for recovery. These experts agree that the longer an anorexic waits to get help, the harder it will be to fully recover.

The outlook for bulimics is far better. *Consumers' Research* suggests that "about 50% of all women initially diagnosed with bulimia were free of their symptoms after five to 10 years, regardless of whether or not they received treatment."[71] Doctors are unsure why some bulimics recover from their illness on their own. Perhaps, experts suggest, some simply outgrow the need to conform to culture's idea of beauty. Others may overcome the stresses of family, school, or work, and still others may simply learn to accept themselves and their bodies. One woman who became danger-ously thin in her teens and early twenties and eventually recov-ered on her own says, "I began to let up on myself and noticed a kind voice inside [my] critical head."[72] She began to feel attractive, independent, and capable. Friends and family also encouraged her to take pleasure in eating rather than worry that what she ate would cause her to become fat. In time and with support she was able to change her attitude about food, and about her destructive behavior.

Chapter 6

Preventing Anorexia and Bulimia

Sɪɴᴄᴇ ɴᴏ ᴍᴇᴅɪᴄᴀʟ cure for anorexia and bulimia has been discovered, doctors have no clear-cut method for preventing these disorders. Therefore, to date the best method available for preventing eating disorders lies in building public awareness. By educating teens, parents, teachers, coaches, the media, and the medical community about the possible causes and, above all, the physical dangers of anorexia and bulimia, experts believe that the number of cases can be reduced.

The Media

Some experts believe that the best way to battle eating disorders is to battle the cultural messages that equate being thin with being beautiful. In fact, some advocates are attempting to change the way advertisers market their products—and they're succeeding. For example, Mary Baures, Psy.D., a psychotherapist in Danvers, Massachusetts, founded a group called Boycott Anorexic Marketing (BAM) in an effort to take aim against companies that use ultrathin models in their advertising campaigns. By boycotting certain products, the members of BAM were able to convince some companies to stop featuring the ultrathin in their ads. Companies such as Kellogg and Coca-Cola, for example, switched from skinny models to sporty models as a way to promote both their products and good physical health. In this way, BAM is helping to change how the media portrays—and how the public perceives—beauty.

Media coverage of eating disorders has increased as well. Numerous articles have appeared in magazines aimed at teens and at parents. Many of these articles feature real-life accounts of people who suffer from anorexia and bulimia and are a positive step toward educating the public about the dangers of these illnesses.

The purpose of such articles, of course, is to steer teens away from anorexia and bulimia. However, in some cases, the opposite occurs. Media efforts to educate people about eating disorders may actually serve to glamorize these illnesses by exposing teens to possibilities for weight control that they may not have otherwise considered. In addition, sometimes news reports of celebrities who suffer from anorexia and bulimia focus on the individual and not on the illness. This leaves teens

with an impression of the beautiful celebrity rather than the physical danger involved. Some experts worry, then, that these reports fail to communicate the serious consequences of eating disorders and may prompt a teen to follow in the celebrities' footsteps.

In addition to advertisers' ultrathin models and news about anorexic and bulimic celebrities, teens are bombarded by ads for diet products. New products to help people lose weight constantly flood the consumer market, and fad diets continually hit the newsstands. Foods advertised as lowfat and nonfat line the supermarket shelves. On top of all that, restaurants, fast-food establishments, and food manufacturers continually pressure the public to indulge their ever-growing appetites. Yet the impression remains that a quick-fix for overeating is readily available thanks to the countless diet products. What the public does not know, however, is that dieting often backfires, and those who diet can be caught in a dangerous yo-yo cycle of losing and gaining weight. Some experts even go so far as to point to this yo-yo pattern as the main cause of anorexia and bulimia.

The Diet Myth

Dispelling these diet myths and educating the public about proper nutrition are key factors in preventing anorexia and bulimia. Dieting throws off the body's natural balance. So when a person cuts back on calories to lose weight, the body naturally adjusts. According to Beatrice Trum Hunter of *Consumers' Research,* "The body adjusts itself to run on fewer calories, and it becomes more efficient in using the available calories in order to conserve its nutrient reserves."[73] This natural adaptation can hinder weight loss, however, because dieters usually experience an initial decrease in weight, but their weight often plateaus (levels off) once their body has made the adjustment, meaning they stop shedding pounds. This leads to frustration.

When dieters reach this point they often quit the diet and resume their normal eating habits. Since the body has adapted

Diet products offering a quick-fix can backfire causing the dieter to gain back even more weight than was lost.

to fewer calories, though, it is now programmed to store any extra calories as fat. Because of this, many dieters actually gain back more weight than they lost. This leads to even more frustration.

One ballerina, for example, who had reached 150 pounds—considered normal for an average girl of nearly six feet but too heavy for a ballerina—began throwing up and taking up to thirty laxatives after each meal in an effort to be thinner. She still didn't lose weight fast enough, so she began to starve herself, and the weight still didn't come off. She didn't understand that her body's metabolism had slowed to the point that losing weight became more and more difficult. Ultimately she became so frustrated and sick that she had to give up dancing altogether, claiming, "Ballet wasn't an art form anymore, it was a power struggle between me and my weight."[74] After being treated for her eating disorder and learning to eat three nutritious meals a day, the ballerina was able to return to a normal weight. In fact, she stabilized at 125 pounds, a healthy weight. This was a result of properly balanced meals, further proof that dieting is not the key to weight loss.

Athletes: A Special Case of Prevention

In the case of the ballerina, as in the case of any athlete who suffers from an eating disorder, special circumstances exist. Therefore, prevention of eating disorders among athletes involves other factors that do not affect the general population. An athlete who suffers from an eating disorder is most likely part of a high school, university, or professional sports program. Therefore, coaches and administrators are thought to have a special responsibility to make sure their athletes are healthy. Yet Barbara Bickford, an attorney and assistant professor of exercise and sport science at the University of North Carolina at Chapel Hill, believes that many sports programs allow athletes to put their health at risk. Sara Hoffman Jurand, who interviewed Bickford, reports, "Many coaches and administrators ignore the problems, possibly because they consider it a woman's issue or do not think they should become involved in athletes' personal lives."[75]

Such disregard concerns experts who stress that athletic department personnel should be educated about eating disorders as well as their symptoms and warning signs. Department personnel should know, Bickford and others contend, what steps to take if an athlete develops symptoms of an eating disorder. These steps should include prompt treatment by a physician or

Experts feel that eating disorders can be prevented in young adult athletes by coaches and administrators who can watch for symptoms and warning signs and teach proper diet and nutrition.

a psychologist trained in treating eating disorders. Athletes should also be schooled in proper diet and nutrition and be told about the health risks of improper weight loss. Jurand says, "By addressing the growing problem, coaches, trainers, and administrators can protect not only their schools, but also their athletes' well-being."[76]

Christy Henrich's case was one that prompted the USA Gymnastics Federation to help prevent eating disorders among its athletes. According to Merrell Noden, the federation began by measuring the bone density of its team members and found three who had a deficiency. The reporter says, "It [the federation] says it is trying to teach young gymnasts that they can say no if they feel too much is being asked by a coach."[77] Parents and friends are also encouraged to complain to the federation if they suspect that a member has an eating disorder.

Warning Signs

Although understanding the warning signs of an eating disorder is not a means of prevention, it is a way to stop anorexia and bulimia before they become life-threatening. Anorexics might wear baggy clothing or become obsessed with food: reading recipes; shopping for food; and cooking for others. They might embark on a rigorous exercise routine or compulsively count calories. Martha's friend remembers an incident at the mall. "We spent twenty minutes going back and forth between these two frozen-yogurt stores while Martha figured out which flavor had the least fat."[78] Anorexics might also begin to

---

Warning Signs of Bulimia

▶ Frequent bingeing or eating uncontrollably

▶ Purging after a binge by fasting, excessive exercise, vomiting, or abusing laxatives or diuretics

▶ Using the bathroom frequently after meals

▶ Preoccupation with body weight

▶ Depression or mood swings

▶ Irregular menstrual periods

▶ Development of dental problems, swollen cheeks/ glands, heartburn and/or bloating

▶ Experiencing personal or family problems with drugs or alcohol

Source: The American Anorexia/Bulimia Association, Inc.

lie. Martha, for example, swore her friend to secrecy about the yogurt and then lied to her mother about what she had for lunch.

Bulimics exhibit other warning signs. Whereas anorexics frequently excuse themselves from meals, claiming that they already ate, bulimics excuse themselves *after* meals, hurrying to the bathroom to purge in private. They may also begin to develop antisocial behavior as they try harder and harder to hide their problem. For example, because they often binge on large quantities of food, they may choose to eat in private instead of with friends or family. Some may even decline invitations to parties because they do not want to be tempted by all the food.

These changes in appearance and behavior are usually not immediate. They progress slowly, which means they can be easily overlooked, not only by family and friends but also by medical professionals. Martha recalls, "It's not like one day I just decided, you know what, I think I'm just not going to eat at all. It's more like this long process of digging yourself into a ditch."[79] Similarly, the mother of an anorexic boy remembers that the changes in her son's eating habits were very slow and subtle. They started simply—more fruit, less pizza—and slowly grew into a deadly obsession with food.

What Parents Can Do

Rather than just looking for the warning signs of anorexia and bulimia then, experts advise parents to be proactive in helping teens develop and maintain healthy eating habits and positive attitudes toward food. The Renfrew Center, which specializes in education and treatment for eating disorders, offers tips for parents on its website. The center advises parents to, among other things, examine their own beliefs and behaviors about food and body image and consider how these might influence their children in either a positive or negative way. Parents should also encourage healthy eating and exercise, discuss the dangers of dieting, and allow their children to determine when they are full (as opposed to insisting that children finish what is on their plates). Furthermore,

In addition to teaching healthy eating and exercise habits, parents must be aware of how their own attitudes about food and weight might influence their children.

the center contends, parents should never label foods as "good" or "bad" or use food as a reward or punishment.

Experts also suggest that parents be aware of other influences in their children's environment. For instance, parents can help their children understand that the idealized images of beauty portrayed in the media are not realistic. Mary Baures of Boycott

Anorexic Marketing advises, "[parents should] help their children think more critically about the images they see by explaining that someone in an ad may be unhealthily thin or that there are different kinds of beauty."[80] Equipped with a more critical point of view, most experts contend, teens might be inclined to question the ad rather than their own appearance.

What Teens Can Do

Teens also can take preventive measures against anorexia and bulimia. This includes becoming aware of their own eating habits. First, doctors advise that teens eat only to satisfy their hunger rather than to satisfy boredom or in response to sadness or anger. Second, they should stop eating when they are full, which requires eating slowly and in moderation. This allows the stomach time to digest and to signal the brain to stop eating. Finally, teens who are unhappy with their appearance should talk about their feelings with an adult rather than engage in "fat talk" with their peers. An adult (a parent, teacher, coach, or school nurse) can provide positive support as well as information about proper nutrition and exercise. Peer groups on the other hand may simply fuel the teen's negative thoughts.

Teens can also take into account how their schedules impact their eating habits. Margo Maine, Ph.D., director of Eating Disorders at the Institute of Living in Hartford, Connecticut, believes that many athletes, in particular, simply don't find time to eat because of hectic and demanding schedules. Others may develop erratic eating habits that don't provide their bodies with the high quality nutrition. The same can be true for teens involved in activities other than sports. Maine says, "Let's say you are a high school student and have a track meet at 1 P.M. You won't eat lunch because you don't want to run with a full stomach, so you end up delaying eating. Then maybe you don't run until 4 P.M. By the time you get home, you're either too exhausted to eat or are past the point of eating."[81] This seemingly innocent behavior can lead to poorer and potentially more destructive eating habits down the road.

The more people know about the dangers, suspected causes, and people most likely to develop eating disorders, the better equipped they will be to prevent the disorders before they arise. Doctors and others, then, hope this awareness will help teens, parents, and others save themselves or someone they know from falling prey to anorexia and bulimia.

Notes

Chapter 1: What Are Anorexia and Bulimia?

1. Joan Jacobs Brumberg, *Fasting Girls: The History of Anorexia Nervosa.* New York: Penguin Books, 1989, p. 18.
2. Beatrice Trum Hunter, "Eating Disorders: Perilous Compulsions," *Consumers' Research,* September 1997, p. 10.
3. Quoted in Leslie N. Vreeland, "Dying to Be Thin—After 30," *Good Housekeeping,* March 1998, p. 137.
4. Quoted in Shannon Brownlee, "Anorexia's Roots in the Brain," *U.S. News & World Report,* August 9, 1999, p. 53.
5. Quoted in David France, "Anorexics Sentenced to Death," *Glamour,* August 1999, p. 215.
6. Quoted in Sabrina Solin, "I Was Dying to Be Thin," *Seventeen,* November 1995, p. 128.
7. Quoted in Brownlee, "Anorexia's Roots in the Brain," p. 52.
8. Quoted in Solin, "I Was Dying to Be Thin," p. 127.
9. Brumberg, *Fasting Girls,* p. 18.
10. Quoted in Alison Bell, "Dying to Win," *Teen,* March 1996, p. 34.
11. Carolyn Costin, *The Eating Disorder Sourcebook.* Los Angeles: Lowell House, 1999, p. 18.
12. Quoted in Daryn Eller, "Detecting Eating Disorders," *Parents,* August 1998, p. 115.
13. Maya Browne, "Dying to be Thin," *Essence,* June 1993, p. 87.
14. Thomas N. Robinson, et al., "Ethnicity and Body Dissatisfaction: Are Hispanic and Asian Girls at Increased Risk for Eating Disorders?" *Journal of Adolescent Health,* December 1996, p. 391.
15. Robinson, et al., "Ethnicity and Body Dissatisfaction," p. 385.

16. Jean Seligmann, et al., "The Pressure to Lose," *Newsweek*, May 2, 1994, p. 60.

17. Quoted in Seligmann, "The Pressure to Lose," p. 61.

18. Quoted in Renee Despres, "Burn, Baby, Burn," *Women's Sports + Fitness*, May 1997, p. 40.

19. Merrell Noden, "Dying to Win," *Sports Illustrated*, August 8, 1994, p. 58.

20. Bell, "Dying to Win," p. 34.

Chapter 2: Psychological and Biological Causes

21. Quoted in Peggy Claude-Pierre, "Anorexia: A Tale of Two Daughters," *Vogue*, September 1997, p. 672.

22. Quoted in France, "Anorexics Sentenced to Death," p. 213.

23. Lisa Jennifer Selzman, "Starving for Help," *Mademoiselle*, November 1997, p. 197.

24. Costin, *The Eating Disorder Sourcebook*, p. 56.

25. Claude-Pierre, "Anorexia," p. 672.

26. Costin, *The Eating Disorder Sourcebook*, p. 63.

27. Quoted in Solin, "I Was Dying to Be Thin," p. 126.

28. Quoted in Bell, "Dying to Win," p. 38.

29. Costin, *The Eating Disorder Sourcebook*, p. 69.

30. Quoted in Anne Conover Heller, "Is Your Daughter at Risk for an Eating Disorder?" *McCall's*, November 1994, p. 100.

31. Quoted in Hunter, "Eating Disorders," p. 30.

32. Quoted in Heller, "Is Your Daughter at Risk for an Eating Disorder?" p. 96.

33. Judith B. Newman, "Little Girls Who Won't Eat," *Redbook*, October 1997, p. 122.

Chapter 3: Societal Pressures

34. Brumberg, *Fasting Girls*, p. 33.

35. Quoted in Newman, "Little Girls Who Won't Eat," p. 152.

36. Quoted in Jill Neimark, "The Beefcaking of America," *Psychology Today*, November/December 1994, p. 34.

37. Neimark, "The Beefcaking of America," p. 35.

38. Quoted in Eller, "Detecting Eating Disorders," p. 116.

39. Newman, "Little Girls Who Won't Eat," p. 123.

40. Bell, "Dying to Win," p. 35.

41. Quoted in Newman, "Little Girls Who Won't Eat," p. 121.
42. Quoted in Eller, "Detecting Eating Disorders," p. 116.
43. Quoted in Seligmann, "The Pressure to Lose," p. 61.
44. Quoted in Seligmann, "The Pressure to Lose," p. 61.
45. Quoted in Bell, "Dying to Win," p. 34.
46. Quoted in Bell, "Dying to Win," p. 38.
47. *Newsweek*, "Fat-Phobia in the Fijis: TV-Thin Is In," May 31, 1999, p. 70.
48. Hunter, "Eating Disorders," p. 10.

Chapter 4: The Dangers of Eating Disorders

49. Christie Gorman, "Disappearing Act," *Time*, November 2, 1998, p. 110.
50. Quoted in Solin, "I Was Dying to Be Thin," p. 127.
51. Methodist Health Care System, www.methodisthealth.com/womenshealth/hyneamen.htm.
52. Bell, "Dying to Win," p. 40.
53. Costin, *The Eating Disorder Sourcebook*, p. 238.
54. Costin, *The Eating Disorder Sourcebook*, p. 239.
55. Focus Adolescent Services, www.focusas.com/depression.html.
56. Costin, *The Eating Disorder Sourcebook*, p. 217.

Chapter 5: Treatment and Recovery

57. Quoted in Claude-Pierre, "Anorexia," p. 673.
58. Selzman, "Starving for Help," p. 197.
59. Quoted in France, "Anorexics Sentenced to Death," p. 214.
60. Selzman, "Starving for Help," p. 197.
61. Quoted in France, "Anorexics Sentenced to Death," p. 215.
62. Quoted in France, "Anorexics Sentenced to Death," p. 214.
63. Quoted in Despres, "Burn, Baby, Burn," p. 41.
64. Quoted in Despres, "Burn, Baby, Burn," p. 41.
65. Quoted in *Psychology Today*, "Breaking the Dieting Habit," March/April 1995, p. 12.
66. Solin, "I Was Dying to Be Thin," p. 127.
67. Lauren M. Frasciello and Susan G. Willard, "Anorexia Nervosa in Males: A Case Report," *Clinical Social Work Journal*, Spring 1995, p. 53.
68. Selzman, "Starving for Help," p. 197.

69. Quoted in Karen Goldberg Goff, "Research Ties Bulimia, Anorexia to Genetics," *Washington Times*, April 2, 2000, http:\\ proquest.umi.com.

70. Vreeland, "Dying to Be Thin—After 30," p. 138.

71. Hunter, "Eating Disorders," p. 12.

72. Quoted in Dorothy Foltz-Gray, "When My Son Stopped Eating," *Health*, October 1998, p. 111.

Chapter 6: Preventing Anorexia and Bulimia

73. Hunter, "Eating Disorders," p. 11.

74. Quoted in Bell, "Dying to Win," p. 36.

75. Sara Hoffman Jurand, "Colleges May Be Liable for Athletes' Eating Disorders, Report Says," *Trial*, May 2000, p. 101.

76. Jurand, "Colleges May Be Liable," p. 101.

77. Noden, "Dying to Win," p. 60.

78. Quoted in Solin, "I Was Dying to Be Thin," p. 126.

79. Quoted in Solin, "I Was Dying to Be Thin," p. 126.

80. Quoted in Eva Pomice, "I'm So Fat: When Kids Hate Their Bodies," *Redbook*, April 1995, p. 188.

81. Quoted in Bell, "Dying to Win," p. 38.

Organizations to Contact

Academy for Eating Disorders (AED)
6728 Old McLean Village Drive
McLean, VA 22101
(703) 556-9222
www.acadeatdis.org/

The Academy for Eating Disorders (AED) offers basic information on eating disorders as well as resources for professionals such as newsletters, links, and conference information.

American Anorexia Bulimia Association, Inc. (AABA)
165 West 46th Street, Suite 1108
New York, NY 10036
(212) 575-6200
www.aabainc.org/home.html

The American Anorexia Bulimia Association, Inc. (AABA) offers help-lines, referral networks, public information, school outreach, media support, professional training, support groups, and prevention programs.

Anorexia Nervosa and Related Eating Disorders, Inc. (ANRED)
P.O. Box 5102
Eugene, OR 97405
(503) 344-1144
www.anred.com/

The Anorexia Nervosa and Related Eating Disorders, Inc. (ANRED) website offers general information as well as statistics, warning signs, causes, treatment, and recovery.

Caring Online
www.caringonline.com/

Caring Online features news about eating disorders, legislative developments, biological causes, body image issues, therapies, and many links.

Eating Disorders Awareness & Prevention, Inc.
603 Stewart Street, Suite 803
Seattle, WA 98101
(206) 382-3587
www.members.aol.com/edapinc/home.html

Eating Disorders Awareness & Prevention, Inc. sponsors Eating Disorders Awareness Week in February with a network of state coordinators and education programs.

Eating Disorder Referral and Information Center
www.edreferral.com/

This international referral organization is dedicated to the prevention and treatment of eating disorders. It provides information and local treatment resources for all forms of eating disorders.

National Association of Anorexia Nervosa and Associated Disorders (ANAD)
P.O. Box 7
Highland Park, IL 60035
Hotline: (847) 831-3438
Fax: (847) 433-4632
www.anad.org/

The National Association of Anorexia Nervosa and Associated Disorders (ANAD) offers free hotline counseling and operates an international network of support groups for people who suffer from eating disorders. ANAD publishes a quarterly newsletter; provides educational speakers, programs, and presentations for schools, colleges, public health agencies, and community groups; and offers referrals to health care professionals.

The Renfrew Center

www.renfrew.org

The Renfrew Center provides education and treatment for anorexia, bulimia, and compulsive overeating as well as trauma, anxiety, depression, and women's issues at centers in New York, Pennsylvania, Florida, and Connecticut. Information, useful links, and expert advice are also available on their website.

For Further Reading

Books

Janet Bode, *Food Fight: A Guide to Eating Disorders for Pre-Teens and Their Parents*. New York: Simon & Schuster, 1997. This book focuses on advice both for teens who suffer from eating disorders and their parents. It includes checklists of triggers, practical suggestions for helping individuals regain control of their eating habits, and nutritional information. The reading level of this book is preteen (ages 9–12).

Jenny Bryan, *Eating Disorders*. Austin, TX: Rainstree Steck-Vaughn Publishers, 2000. Written by a medical journalist, the book covers anorexia, bulimia, and compulsive eating, including why people develop eating disorders and what can be done to help them.

Ellen Erlanger, *Eating Disorders: A Question and Answer Book About Anorexia Nervosa and Bulimia Nervosa*. Minneapolis: Lerner Publications, 1988. This book discusses the characteristics and causes of these disorders as well as the damage these disorders can do to a person's body and emotional well-being.

Michael Maloney and Rachel Kranz, *Straight Talk About Eating Disorders*. New York: Facts On File, 1991. This book defines anorexia, bulimia, and compulsive eating and looks at the social and biological factors involved in each of these disorders. It includes personal accounts from people who have these disorders.

Paul R. Robbins, *Anorexia and Bulimia*. Springfield, NJ: Enslow Publications, 1998. The book discusses anorexia, bulimia, and binge eating, including the history of the disorders, their symptoms, possible causes, prevention, treatment, and real-life accounts of young people who have experienced the disorders.

Works Consulted

Books

Arnold Andersen, *Making Weight: Men's Conflicts with Food.* Carlsbad, CA: Gurze Books, 2000. Director of the Eating Disorder Program at the University of Iowa College of Medicine, Andersen is an authority on male eating disorders. The book discusses concerns about food, weight, body image, and exercise that are specific to males.

Hilde Bruch, *The Golden Cage: The Enigma of Anorexia Nervosa.* New York: Vintage Books, 1979. The author presents case studies from her own practice, which give a vivid picture of the possible causes of anorexia, its effects, and methods of treatment.

Joan Jacobs Brumberg, *Fasting Girls: The History of Anorexia Nervosa.* New York: Penguin Books, 1989. Anorexia Nervosa became the focus of this author's professional research when she joined the Department of Human Development and Family Studies at Cornell University as its resident historian. This highly academic work maps the history of anorexia nervosa from the 1300s through the 1900s with meticulous research and an eye toward society's evolving attitudes toward food, religion, medicine, and feminism.

Carolyn Costin, *The Eating Disorder Sourcebook.* Los Angeles: Lowell House, 1999. This book provides the most current information about the causes, identification, treatment, and prevention of eating disorders. The author writes from personal experience and as a medical professional with twenty years' experience as a specialist in the field of eating disorders.

Roberta Trattner Sherman and Ron A. Thompson, *Bulimia, a Guide for Family and Friends.* San Francisco: Jossey-Bass Publishers,

1990. The authors are founders and codirectors of the Eating Disorders Program at Bloomington Hospital in Indiana. The book covers the behaviors, thoughts, and emotions specific to bulimia in addition to the role of society, the role of the family, and individual factors.

Periodicals and Internet Sources

Liz Applegate, "Running into Trouble," *Runner's World*, April 1998.

Alison Bell, "Dying to Win," *Teen*, March 1996.

Maya Browne, "Dying to Be Thin," *Essence*, June 1993.

Shannon Brownlee, "Anorexia's Roots in the Brain," *U.S. News & World Report*, August 9, 1999.

Peggy Claude-Pierre, "Anorexia: A Tale of Two Daughters," *Vogue*, September 1997.

Renee Despres, "Burn, Baby, Burn," *Women's Sports + Fitness*, May 1997.

Daryn Eller, "Detecting Eating Disorders," *Parents*, August 1998.

Focus Adolescent Services, www. focusas.com/depression.html.

Dorothy Foltz-Gray, "When My Son Stopped Eating," *Health*, October 1998.

David France, "Anorexics Sentenced to Death," *Glamour*, August 1999.

Lauren M. Frasciello and Susan G. Willard, "Anorexia Nervosa in Males: A Case Report," *Clinical Social Work Journal*, Spring 1995.

Karen Goldberg Goff, "Research Ties Bulimia, Anorexia to Genetics," *Washington Times*, April 2, 2000, http:\\proquest. umi.com.

Christine Gorman, "Disappearing Act," *Time*, November 2, 1998.

Anne Conover Heller, "Is Your Daughter at Risk for an Eating Disorder?" *McCall's*, November 1994.

Beatrice Trum Hunter, "Eating Disorders: Perilous Compulsions," *Consumers' Research*, September 1997.

Sara Hoffman Jurand, "Colleges May Be Liable for Athletes' Eating Disorders, Report Says," *Trial,* May 2000.

Rodolfo R. Llinas, "The Rhythm of Mind," *Discover,* January 2000.

Methodist Health Care Systems, www.methodisthealth.com/womenshealth/hyneamen.htm.

Jill Neimark, "The Beefcaking of America," *Psychology Today,* November/December 1994.

Judith B. Newman, "Little Girls Who Won't Eat," *Redbook,* October 1997.

Newsweek, "Fat-Phobia in the Fijis: TV-Thin Is In," May 31, 1999.

Merrell Noden, "Dying to Win," *Sports Illustrated,* August 8, 1994.

Eva Pomice, "I'm So Fat: When Kids Hate Their Bodies," *Redbook,* April 1995.

Psychology Today, "Breaking the Dieting Habit," March/April 1995.

Renfrew Center, www.renfrew.org.

Thomas N. Robinson, et al., "Ethnicity and Body Dissatisfaction: Are Hispanic and Asian Girls at Increased Risk for Eating Disorders?" *Journal of Adolescent Health,* December 1996.

Jean Seligmann, et al., "The Pressure to Lose," *Newsweek,* May 2, 1994.

Lisa Jennifer Selzman, "Starving for Help," *Mademoiselle,* November 1997.

Sabrina Solin, "I Was Dying to Be Thin," *Seventeen,* November 1995.

Ron A. Thompson and Roberta Trattner Sherman, "Athletes, Athletic Performance, and Eating Disorders: Healthier Alternatives," *Journal of Social Issues,* 1999.

Leslie N. Vreeland, "Dying to Be Thin—After 30," *Good Housekeeping,* March 1998.

B. Timothy Walsh and Michael J. Devlin, "Eating Disorders: Progress and Problems," *Science,* May 29, 1998.

Index

Picture Credits

About the Author

Alison Cotter earned a bachelor's in marketing from Syracuse University and is currently pursuing a master's of fine arts in creative writing at California State University in Long Beach. She worked as a director of communications for Los Angeles's leading performing arts center and now specializes in marketing, public relations, and fundraising as a freelance writer. This is her first book for Lucent Books. She lives in Long Beach with her husband, daughter, and a dog named Slugger.